# PAPER PIECE A
# *MERRY CHRISTMAS*

⫸⫸⫸ Jodie Davis ⫷⫷⫷

*Martingale*
& COMPANY

BOTHELL, WASHINGTON

## ACKNOWLEDGMENTS

*Thanks to Kathy Semone, for piecing and quilting most of the blocks and quilts presented in this book; and to Glenda Irvine, for bringing inspiration—and herself—from Florida just in time to help me design "Peace on Earth."*

⇒⇒⇒⇐⇐⇐

## DEDICATION

*To Santa Claus, for giving us the opportunity to believe in and celebrate the strength and goodness of the human spirit.*

### CREDITS

President . . . . . . . . . . . . . . . . . . . . . . . . . . . . . . Nancy J. Martin
CEO . . . . . . . . . . . . . . . . . . . . . . . . . . . . . . . Daniel J. Martin
Publisher . . . . . . . . . . . . . . . . . . . . . . . . . . . . . Jane Hamada
Editorial Director . . . . . . . . . . . . . . . . . . . . . . Mary V. Green
Editorial Project Manager . . . . . . . . . . . . . . . . . . .Tina Cook
Technical Editor . . . . . . . . . . . . . . . . . . . . . . . . . Laurie Baker
Copy Editor . . . . . . . . . . . . . . . . . . . . . . . . . . . Ellen Balstad
Design and Production Manager . . . . . . . . . . . . . . . . . . Stan Green
Illustrator . . . . . . . . . . . . . . . . . . . . . . . . . . . . . Laurel Strand
Photographer . . . . . . . . . . . . . . . . . . . . . . . . . . . . Brent Kane
Cover Designer . . . . . . . . . . . . . . . . . . . . . Magrit Baurecht
Text Designer . . . . . . . . . . . . . . . . . . . . . . . . . . .Trina Stahl

That Patchwork Place is an imprint of Martingale & Company.

Paper Piece a Merry Christmas
© 2000 by Jodie Davis

Martingale & Company
PO Box 118
Bothell, WA 98041-0118 USA
www.patchwork.com

Printed in China
05 04 03 02 01 00 6 5 4 3 2 1

### MISSION STATEMENT

We are dedicated to providing quality products and service by working together to inspire creativity and to enrich the lives we touch.

Library of Congress Cataloging-in-Publication Data

Davis, Jodie.
    Paper piece a Merry Christmas / Jodie Davis.
        p.  cm.
    ISBN 1-56477-296-9
    1. Patchwork—Patterns.  2. Christmas decorations.
3. Miniature quilts.  I. Title.

TT835.D374697 2000
746.46'041—dc21

00-035510

# CONTENTS

# INTRODUCTION

THIS BOOK IS a collection of paper-piecing patterns and quilt projects. With forty-six Christmas-theme quilt blocks and border patterns, plus complete instructions for ten wonderful little Christmas quilts, *Paper Piece a Merry Christmas* is a reference and project book in one.

To begin, I start you out with a complete chapter on paper piecing that also includes instructions for finishing your quilt. All you need is the ability to sew on a straight line.

Following the paper-piecing primer, forty-six block and border designs are featured. Each design is presented full size, with a photo to show you how the block looks when it is finished.

The projects are featured next. Carefully illustrated, step-by-step instructions and materials lists make each quilt easy to assemble. Plus, I've added simple instructions to turn your blocks into adorable ornaments to decorate your holiday tree or use as package tie-ons.

And finally, don't miss "Resources" on pages 94–96. In addition to devotedly visiting local quilting stores, I am always on the lookout for new mail-order resources, especially those with Web sites. These gems I share are tried and true and are sure to spark your creative muse with their wonderful offerings.

Now let's get those sewing machines humming!

# PAPER-PIECING PRIMER

IF YOU CAN sew on a straight line, you can create any of the projects in this book using the paper-piecing techniques presented in this chapter. Paper piecing is a fun and accurate way to piece blocks, but you do need to think a little differently than when you are doing traditional quilting. In fact, you need to think backward because you piece the blocks from the wrong side of the patterns. If you have not tried paper piecing, this may sound a little crazy, but once you try it, I guarantee that you will be amazed at how easy it is to do.

## Defining the Pattern Markings

THE PATTERNS for the blocks in this book are found on pages 15–60. They are full size with ¼" seam allowances added. As you look at each pattern, you will notice several things:

✶ Each pattern consists of at least one part. If the pattern has more than one part, each part is labeled with a letter. Parts are pieced separately and then joined together in the letter order indicated in "Joining Sequence," which appears on the same page as the pattern.

* Each part is divided into sections, and each section is numbered. The numbers indicate the sewing sequence for the fabric pieces.

* Each pattern has dashed and solid lines. Dashed lines represent cutting lines and solid lines represent sewing lines.

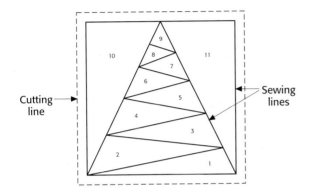

Cutting line

Sewing lines

* Some patterns are the mirror image of the block you see in the photo. This is because the blocks are sewn from the marked side of the paper foundation, which is the wrong side of the finished block. For symmetrical blocks, the patterns and finished blocks look the same, but for asymmetrical blocks, the finished blocks are mirror images of the patterns.

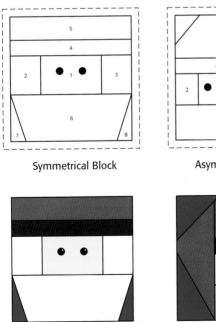
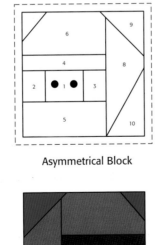

Symmetrical Block     Asymmetrical Block

## Selecting a Foundation Material

THE BLOCK patterns for the quilts in this book need to be traced onto some sort of a foundation material. The foundation provides sewing lines and stability for sewing and piecing the blocks together. It can be either permanent or temporary, depending upon the desired end result, or whether you plan to work by hand or machine.

Permanent foundations are usually made of fabric. They remain in the completed quilt, adding an extra layer. If you choose to use permanent foundations, select a lightweight fabric such as muslin, batiste, or broadcloth, which can be seen through for tracing but is strong enough to add stability to the blocks.

Temporary foundations, in contrast to permanent foundations, are removed before completing the quilt, reducing the amount of bulk in the seams. Many types of paper can be used as temporary foundations. Newsprint is the most economical, but slightly more expensive materials such as tracing paper and vellum offer important characteristics that make the additional cost worthwhile. Both are semitransparent, allowing you to see the fabrics through the paper. This is a huge benefit when placing fabric pieces. Also, both tear away from the stitching much easier than regular paper or newsprint. You will appreciate this characteristic when the time comes to remove the paper from your blocks.

## Transferring the Patterns

TO REPRODUCE the block patterns, trace or photocopy them from the book onto a permanent or temporary foundation. Leave about ½" between pattern parts or individual patterns. When tracing, use a ruler to ensure accuracy. Be sure to label each pattern part with the appropriate letter and transfer the piecing sequence numbers to each section. If you choose to use a photocopy machine to reproduce the patterns, watch out for distortion. To test the precision of the copy machine, make one copy of the pattern and measure it to be sure the size matches the original. Once you finish copying the patterns, cut them apart outside the dashed lines if there is more than one pattern part.

Many of the border patterns for the projects presented in this book will need to be lengthened to the size indicated for the quilt. To lengthen a border pattern, trace all but the last section of the pattern and the seam allowances at the ends of the pattern onto foundation material. Shift the foundation to the left so that the last full section lines up with the first full section of the same shape. Continue tracing the border until the desired length is achieved, ending with the last section of the pattern. The project directions will indicate the finished length of the border strip, which *does not* include seam allowances. You can also make multiple photocopies of the border pattern and tape them together to achieve the desired length.

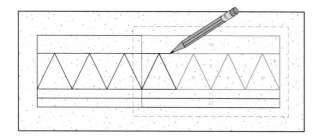

Several of the quilts use mirror images of the block designs. To make a mirror-image block, transfer the design to tracing paper as described above; then turn the paper over and retrace the lines and numbers (reverse the numbers so that they are readable). Transfer the reversed design to the foundation material and mark it with an *M* to indicate that it is a mirror-image pattern.

> ### ⊰⊰⊰ Tip ⊱⊱⊱
>
> Create blocks in any size you desire by using a photocopy machine's enlarging and reducing capabilities. Remember to redraw the seam allowances to 1/4".

### ⊰⊰⊰ Tip ⊱⊱⊱

Color-code or mark your patterns so that you stitch the correct fabric in the proper place. When making multiple blocks, I make an extra copy of the pattern, glue a small piece of the designated fabric in each section, and use it as a key so that I can easily see where the different fabrics go. You can also mark the areas on your foundations with a letter to indicate the desired fabric for each section. For instance, on the foundation for the Dove block in "Peace on Earth," I add a *W* for the white bird pieces and a *B* for blue for the background pieces.

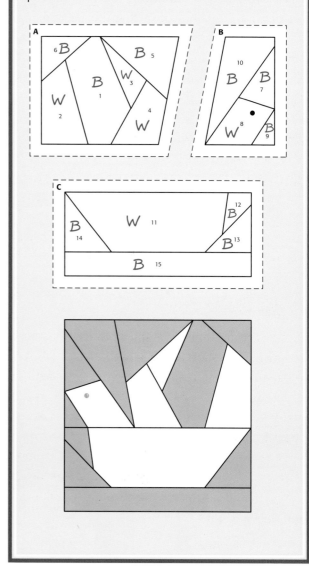

## Cutting the Fabrics

UNLIKE TRADITIONAL piecing, the fabric pieces used in paper piecing do not need to be cut the exact size of the areas they will fill. Simply cut the desired fabric into a chunk that is at least ½" larger on all sides than the area it is to cover. Excess fabric is trimmed away after stitching the piece to the next fabric piece in the sequence. If the piece that is trimmed away is large enough, you can always use it in another area. While this may seem like a waste of fabric, the time saved is well worth it.

One of the beauties of paper piecing is that the foundation stabilizes the fabrics, and as a result, it is unnecessary to follow grain-line rules strictly when cutting fabric. In normal template or rotary-cut piecing, it is imperative that the outside edges of blocks are cut on the straight of grain; if they are cut on the bias, the unstable pieces stretch and cause problems when they are pieced together. There is one caveat, however, with paper piecing. Leave your foundation (if temporary) in place until you sew your blocks together so that the fabric does not stretch. For added protection, I staystitch the outside edge of the quilt top before I remove the paper to prevent the quilt top from distorting before it is bound. Avoid the impulse to use a zigzag stitch around the outside edge. If you do, you will not be able to tear the paper out.

## Preparing to Sew

SET YOUR machine for eighteen to twenty stitches per inch. The short stitch length creates a strong stitch that won't come apart when you tear the paper foundations away, and the closely spaced perforations also facilitate the tearing away of paper foundations.

Choose your thread according to the fabrics selected. Light gray is a good choice for lighter fabrics, while dark gray works well for black prints and darker fabrics.

## Basic Paper Piecing

THE FOLLOWING is a step-by-step overview for paper piecing a block. For information about paper piecing curves, please refer to "Paper Piecing Curved Seams" on page 9.

1. Transfer each part of the desired pattern onto the foundation material.

2. Using a fabric gluestick, apply glue to the right side (unmarked side) of section 1 on the paper foundation. From the fabric indicated for section 1, cut a piece that is at least ½" larger than section 1 on all sides. Place the fabric piece, right side up, over the glued section so that section 1 is completely covered. Press the fabric in place with your hand.

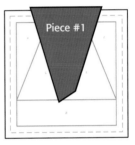

3. Cut a piece of fabric for section 2. With right sides together, place piece 2 against piece 1 so that the majority of piece 2 is over section 1. Leave about ½" of fabric extending into the section marked 2. Working from the marked side of the foundation, stitch along the seam line between section 1 and section 2. Begin and end the stitching several stitches beyond the ends of the line.

Right side of Piece #2

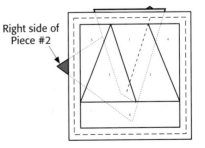

4. Fold down piece 2 to make sure it covers the section marked 2 in the pattern when it is pressed into place. Flip the piece back up and trim the seam allowance to ¼".

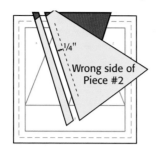

5. Fold piece 2 over the seam and press it in place.

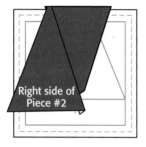

6. Continue to cut and stitch fabric pieces for the remaining sections in the numerical order indicated. Leave at least ½" around the outer edge of each fabric piece for seam allowance.

7. If the block consists of more than one part, complete the remaining parts of each block in the same manner. Add the pieces in numerical order.

8. Lay the part or block, fabric side down (marked paper foundation up), on a cutting mat. Using a rotary cutter and ruler, trim the edges of the block piece(s) along the dashed lines. This leaves a ¼" seam allowance around the block. Make sure you cut through both the foundation and the fabric.

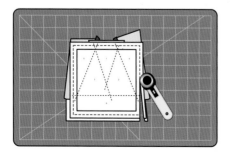

9. To join parts, refer to the instructions in "Joining Sequence" for the block to pin the parts together in the correct order. Stitch along the solid line. Remove the paper *in the seam allowances only.* Press the seam(s) open.

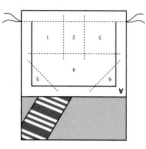

NOTE: *Embellishment details are added after the block or quilt is quilted. Refer to "Details" in the block directions for embellishing each block.*

## ⇛ Tips ⇚

• Though I usually use my ¼" presser foot for all quilt-related sewing, you may find that an open-toe foot helps you see the line as you sew.

• Do not worry about the grain line of the block edges. The paper foundation stabilizes the edges throughout the construction process.

• When pressing, use a hot, dry iron so that you do not distort your block. To avoid shrinking the foundation or getting ink from the foundation onto your iron and your fabric, press only on the fabric side of the blocks.

• To avoid transferring ink from the foundation to your ironing board cover, place a paper towel or piece of felt between the ironing board and the block.

## Paper Piecing Curved Seams

To PIECE the Holly block on page 31, you will need to use a slightly different paper-piecing technique—curved piecing. Because the seams are curved, the fabric can't lie flat. Therefore, the excess fabric has to be pleated.

The following steps explain the process of paper piecing curves.

1. Follow steps 1–4 of "Basic Paper Piecing" on pages 7–8 to prepare the block and stitch the first 2 pieces together along the curved line. To allow for pleating the excess fabric, cut the fabric pieces for sections 2–7 approximately 1" larger than you would for normal paper piecing.

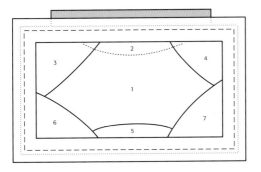

2. Fold piece 2 over the seam. Fold 2 pleats, either toward or away from the center, into the curved fabric piece to make it lie flat. It does not matter which way you fold the fabric as long as you are consistent, folding the pleats the same way in each quilt block. Fold the pleats one at a time, placing a pin in each pleat as you go.

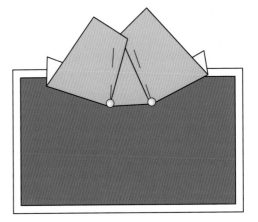

3. In the same manner, add the remaining curved sections in numerical order.

4. Working on the marked side of the paper foundation, machine baste in the seam allowance between the solid and dashed lines to secure the pleats. Remove the pins as you stitch. Use the longest stitch available; you'll be thankful later when you have to tear the stitches out to remove the paper.

5. Using a rotary cutter, trim along the dashed lines.

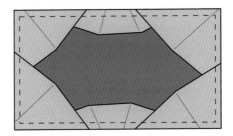

# Finishing Your Quilt

## Assembling the Quilt Top

Now it's time to sew the festive blocks into a quilt top. The following steps explain how.

1. Arrange the finished blocks and any other required fabric pieces in the proper order. Sew them together along the outer solid lines on the foundations in the order indicated in the instructions. Press the seams in the direction specified for each project.

---

### ≫≫ Tips ≪≪

• If there is any doubt regarding how well the block seams will match, baste them together first. If they do not match, you only have to rip out a few basting stitches before and after the seam match to make the adjustment; then you can resew the entire seam with a normal stitch length.

• Try using vinyl-coated paper clips instead of pins to hold your blocks together for stitching.

---

2. Stitch the side borders to the quilt sides. Press the seam allowances in the direction indicated in the quilt instructions. Stitch the top and bottom borders to the top and bottom edges. Press the seam allowances in the direction indicated in the quilt instructions.

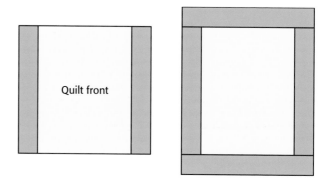

Quilt front

3. Remove the paper foundation from the backs of the blocks. To do so, gently tear the paper as if you were tearing stamps. A gentle tug against the seam will give you a head start in loosening the paper foundation from the stitching.

4. Press the completed quilt top gently, using a dry iron. Lift the iron up and down, rather than dragging it, to avoid distorting the blocks.

---

### ≫≫ Tip ≪≪

You may find a pair of tweezers helpful in removing the foundation. There are always a few pesky little tidbits of paper that remain here and there.

---

## Preparing for Quilting

Before you quilt your project, you must prepare it by marking the top with the quilting design and layering it with backing and batting. Follow steps 1–4 to prepare your quilt and steps 5 and 6 for quilting.

1. Mark the quilt top with the quilting design of your choice.

2. Cut the batting and backing 6" to 8" larger than the quilt top. This will give you 3" to 4" extra on each side of the quilt.

3. Lay the backing, wrong side up, on a flat surface. Place the batting over the backing. Center the quilt top, right side up, on top of the batting and backing.

4. Working from the center out, baste the layers of the quilt "sandwich" together with thread or safety pins.

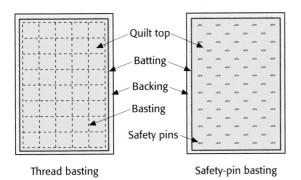

Thread basting       Safety-pin basting

> ≫≫ Tip ≪≪
>
> Try one of the new basting sprays to hold the quilt layers together. These products temporarily hold the quilt layers together without the use of any other form of basting. Just be sure to use the spray in a well-ventilated area.

5. Quilt the top as desired.

6. Remove all basting stitches or any remaining safety pins when you are finished quilting.

## Making and Applying Binding

Binding is the last bastion of handwork remaining in quilting for those of us who have embraced the sewing machine so completely. Even though I use the sewing machine for most of my quilting, it gives me great satisfaction to sit down in the evening and actually finish a quilt by hand.

Because these are small quilts and will not suffer heavy use like a bed quilt, I have economized on fabric by using binding strips cut on the straight of grain rather than the bias grain. To make straight-grain binding, simply cut 2"-wide strips from the lengthwise or crosswise grain of the fabric. Join the ends together to make one long, continuous strip.

Once you have made your binding strips, apply the binding. Use either the overlapped corner method or the mitered corner method. Bind each quilt using the desired method or as specified in the quilt project directions.

### Binding with Overlapped Corners

1. Trim the backing and batting even with the quilt top.

2. With wrong sides together, press the binding strip in half lengthwise.

3. Measure the length of the quilt sides. From the binding strip, cut 2 strips that are the same length as each side plus approximately 2". With right sides together and raw edges matching, stitch the 2 binding strips to the sides of the quilt. Allow approximately 1" of excess binding at each end. Use a ¼" seam allowance. Trim the ends even with the upper and lower edges.

Quilt front

4. Fold the binding to the back of the quilt over the raw edges of the quilt "sandwich," covering the machine stitching. Slipstitch the binding in place.

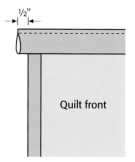

Quilt back

5. Measure the length of the top and bottom edges of the quilt. From the remaining binding strip, cut 2 strips that are the same length as the top and bottom edges plus approximately 2". Stitch the strips to the top and bottom edges in the same manner as the side binding strips, allowing approximately 1" excess binding at each end. Trim the ends of the unfinished binding ½" longer than the bound side edges.

½"

Quilt front

6. Working on the back side of the quilt, fold the ends of the top and bottom binding strips over the bound side edges. Fold the binding to the back of the quilt over the raw edges of the quilt "sandwich," covering the machine stitching. Slipstitch the binding in place.

Fold extension.

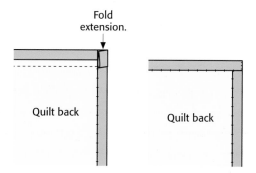

Quilt back

Quilt back

**Binding with Mitered Corners**

1. Trim the batting and backing even with the quilt top.

2. With wrong sides together, press the binding strip in half lengthwise.

3. Place the binding strip along one edge of the right side of the quilt top, matching raw edges. Leaving the first 6" of the binding free, stitch the binding to the quilt. Use a ¼" seam allowance. Stop stitching ¼" from the corner. Backstitch and remove the quilt from the machine.

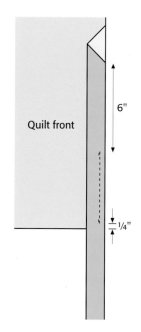

6"

Quilt front

¼"

4. Turn the quilt to prepare to sew the next edge. Fold the binding up, creating a 45°-angle fold.

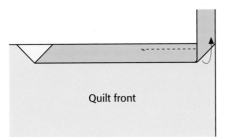

Quilt front

5. Fold the binding down, having the fold even with the top edge of the quilt and the raw edge aligned with the side of the quilt. Beginning at the edge, stitch the binding to the quilt, stopping ¼" from the next corner. Backstitch and remove the quilt from the machine. Continue the folding and stitching process for the remaining corners.

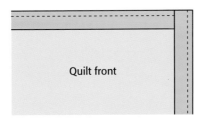

Quilt front

6. When you are within approximately 4" of the starting point, stop stitching. Cut the binding end so it overlaps the unstitched binding at the beginning by at least 5". Pin the ends together 3½" from the starting point. Clip the binding raw edges at the pin mark, being careful not to cut past the seam allowance or into the quilt layers. Open up the binding and match the ends as shown. Stitch the ends together on the diagonal.

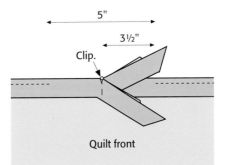

5"

3½"

Clip.

Quilt front

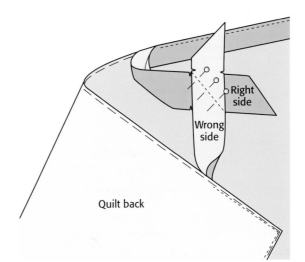

Right side

Wrong side

Quilt back

7. Check to be sure that the binding fits the quilt. Trim off the binding tails and finish stitching the binding to the edge.

8. Fold the binding to the back of the quilt over the raw edges of the quilt "sandwich," covering the machine stitching. Slipstitch the binding in place, mitering the corners.

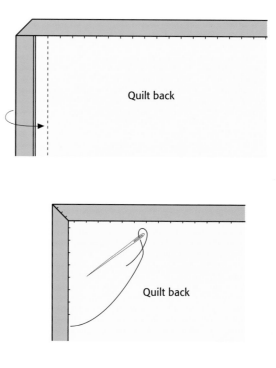

Quilt back

Quilt back

## Santa I

*Finished Size:* 4" x 4"

*Difficulty Level:* Easy

*Details:*

EYES–Stitch ¼"- or ⅜"-diameter buttons to face as indicated.

HAT TIPS–Cut two hat tips from hat fabric.
With right sides together, stitch the pieces together. Leave one edge open. Turn the hat tip right side out, and slip-stitch the opening closed. Position the hat tip upper edge between the dots in the pattern seam allowance. Stitch along the solid line.
Sew a 1"-diameter pompon to the point of the hat tip as indicated.

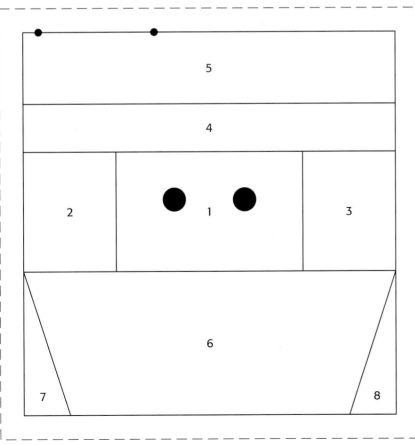

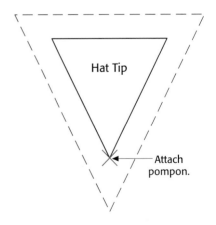

Hat Tip

Attach pompon.

# Santa II

*Finished Size:* 2" x 4"

*Difficulty Level:* Moderate

*Details:*

EYES–Stitch ⅛"-diameter beads to face as indicated.

HAT–Stitch ½"-diameter pompon to hat tip as indicated.

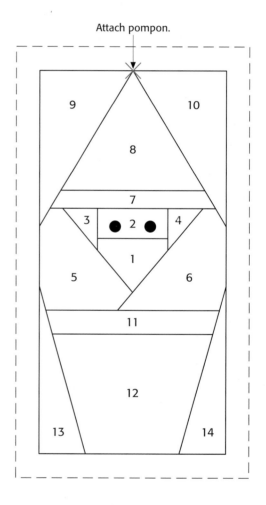

# Santa III

*Finished Size:* 4" x 4"

*Difficulty Level:* Complex

*Joining Sequence:*

B + C = BC

BC + D = BCD

A + BCD = Santa III

*Details:*

EYES–Stitch ⅛"-diameter beads to face as indicated.

HAT–Stitch ½"-diameter pompon to hat tip as indicated.

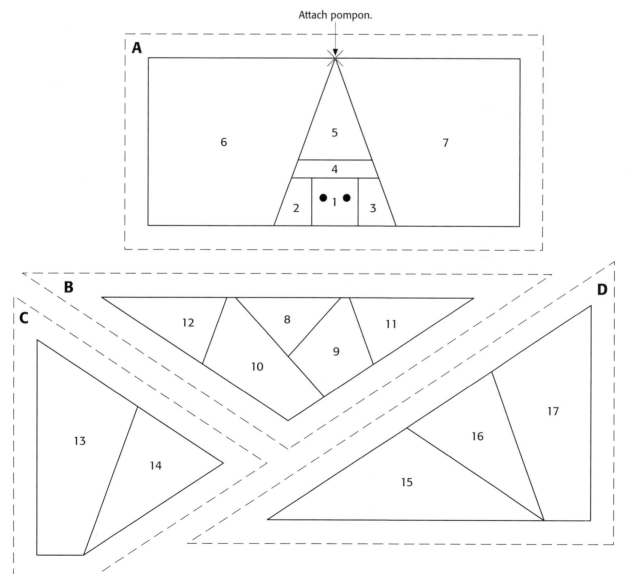

# Santa IV

*Finished Size:* 4" x 4"

*Difficulty Level:* Easy

*Details:*

EYES—Stitch ⅛"- or ¼"-diameter buttons to face as indicated.

HAT—Stitch 1"-diameter pompon to hat tip as indicated.

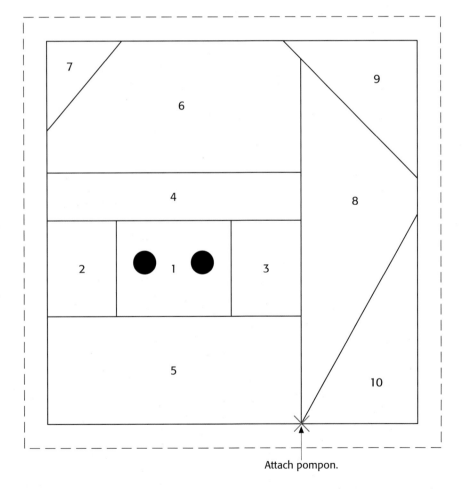

Attach pompon.

# Santa V

*Finished Size:* 4" x 4"

*Difficulty Level:* Moderate

*Joining Sequence:*
A + B = AB
C + D = CD
AB + CD = Santa V

## *Details:*

EYE–Stitch ¼"-diameter button to face as indicated.

HAT–Stitch 1"-diameter pompon to hat tip as indicated.

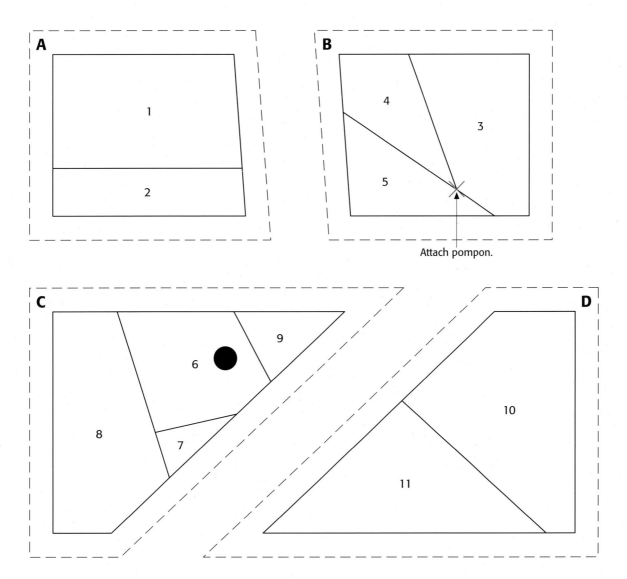

Attach pompon.

# Santa Hat

*Finished Size:* 4" x 4"

*Difficulty Level:* Easy

*Details:*

Hat–Stitch a 1"-diameter pompon to hat tip as indicated.

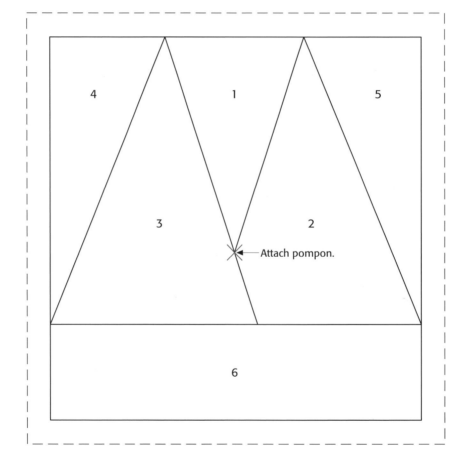

# Wreath

*Finished Size:* 4" x 4"

*Difficulty Level:* Easy

*Details:*

Bow–Stitch ⅝"-wide ribbon to top of wreath and tie into a bow.

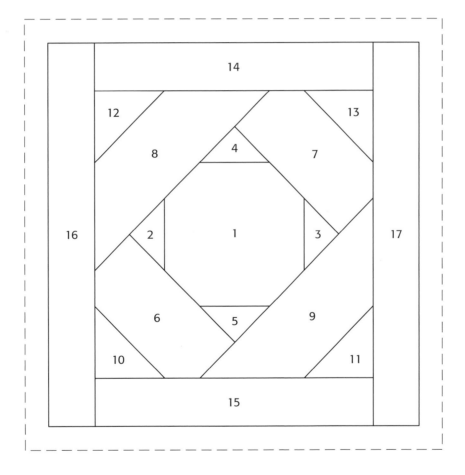

# Cardinal

*Finished Size:* 4" x 4"

*Difficulty Level:* Complex

*Joining Sequence:*

B + C = BC

BC + D = BCD

A + BCD = Cardinal

## Details:

EYE–Stitch ⅛"-diameter button to body as indicated.

LEGS (optional)–Stem stitch with 2 strands of
black floss, or draw with a black,
fine-tip permanent marker.

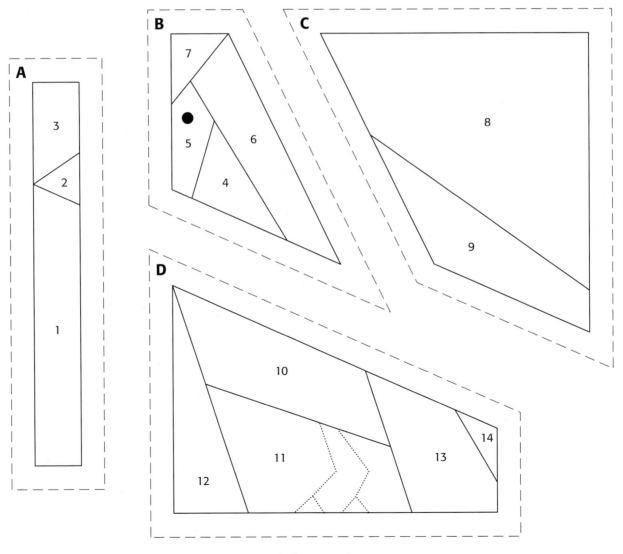

# Candy Cane

*Finished Size:* 2" x 4"

*Difficulty Level:* Easy

*Joining Sequence:*
A + B = Candy Cane

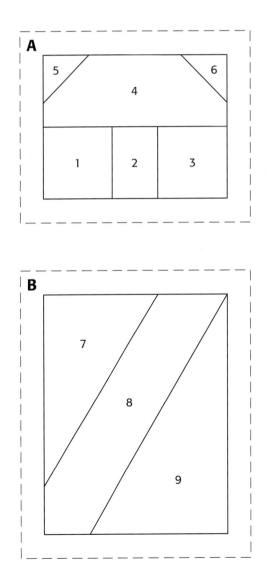

# Christmas Tree I

*Finished Size:* 4" x 4"

*Difficulty Level:* Easy

*Joining Sequence:*
A + B = Christmas Tree I

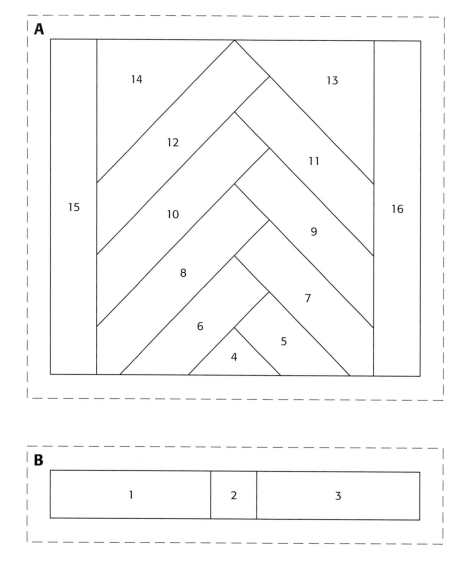

# Christmas Tree II

*Finished Size:* 4" x 4"

*Difficulty Level:* Easy

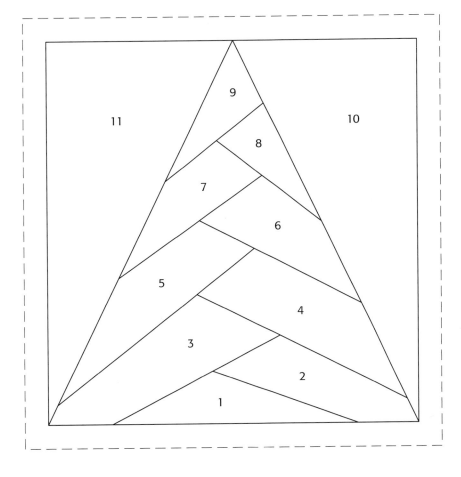

# Christmas Tree III

*Finished Size:* 4" x 4"

*Difficulty Level:* Easy

*Details:*

GOLD STAR–Stitch 1"-diameter button as indicated.

Attach button.

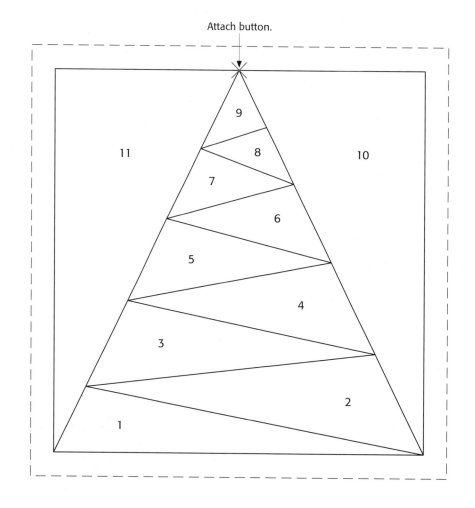

# Bright Star

*Finished Size:* 4" x 4"

*Difficulty Level:* Moderate

*Joining Sequence:*

A + B = AB

ADDITIONAL INSTRUCTIONS—

Make 4 AB pieces and join together as shown.

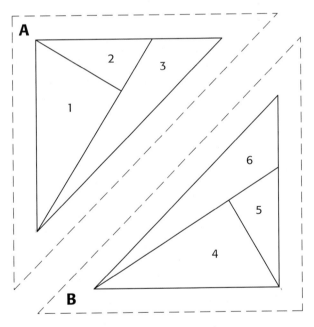

Make 4 of each section.

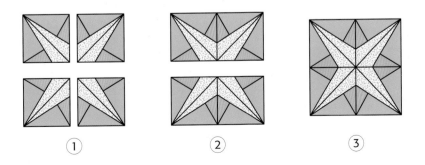

① ② ③

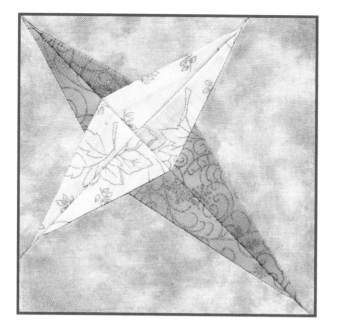

# North Star

*Finished Size:* 4" x 4"

*Difficulty Level:* Complex

*Joining Sequence:*

A + B = AB

C + D = CD

AB + CD = North Star

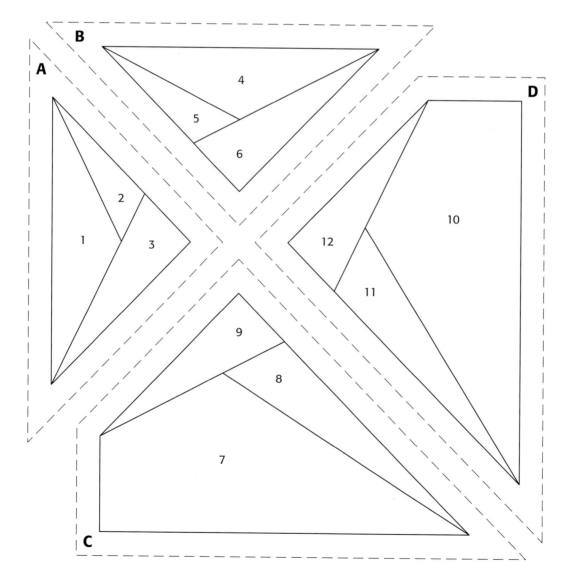

# Christmas Star

*Finished Size:* 4" x 4"

*Difficulty Level:* Moderate

*Joining Sequence:*
B + C = BC
A + BC = ABC
ABC + D = Christmas Star

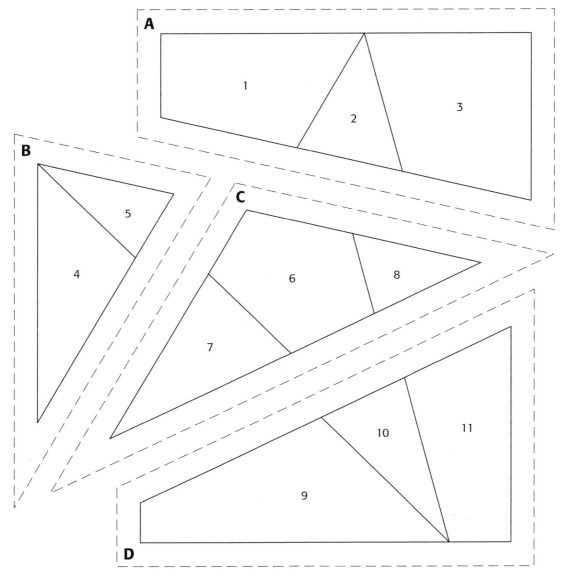

# Sled

*Finished Size:* 4" x 4"

*Difficulty Level:* Moderate

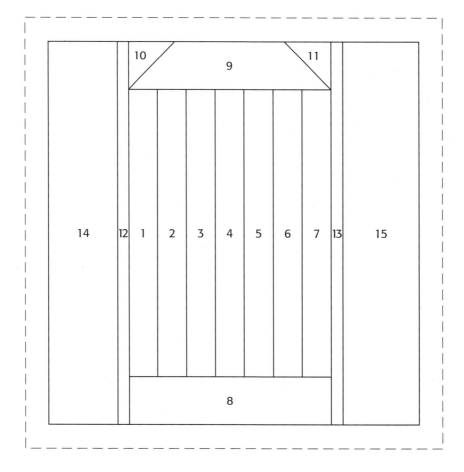

# Holly

*Finished Size:* 2" x 4"

*Difficulty Level:* Easy

*Details:*

BERRY—Stitch ½"-diameter red button as indicated.

ADDITIONAL INSTRUCTIONS—Refer to "Paper Piecing Curved Seams" on page 9.

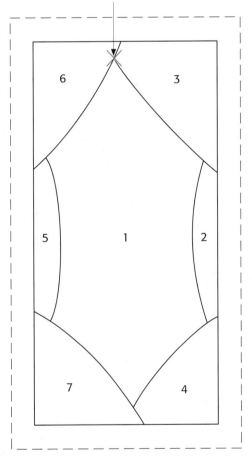

Attach button.

# $Bow$

*Finished Size:* 4" x 4"

*Difficulty Level:* Complex

*Joining Sequence:*
A + B = AB
AB + C = ABC
ABC + D = Bow

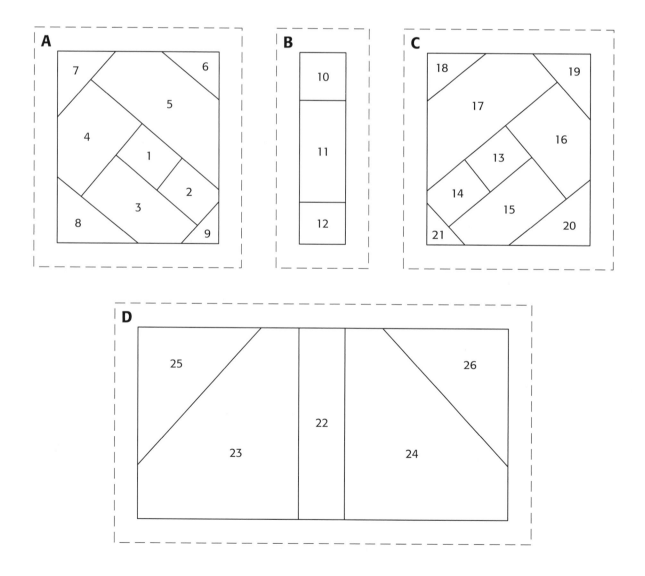

# Rocking Horse

*Finished Size:* 4" x 4"

*Difficulty Level:* Moderate

*Joining Sequence:*

A + B = AB

AB + C = Rocking Horse

*Details:*

EYES—Stitch ⅛"-diameter bead or button to head as indicated.

TAIL AND MANE—Stitch imitation hair to tail and mane sections.

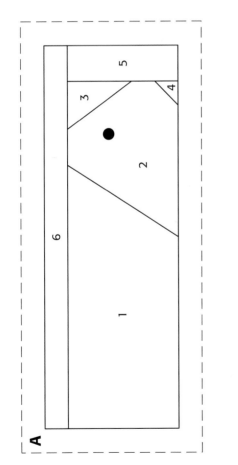

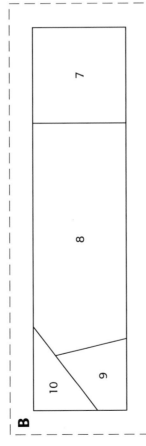

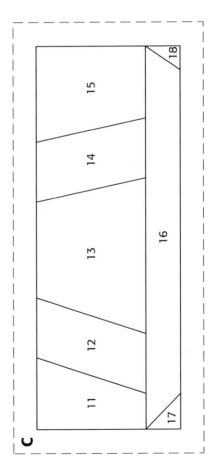

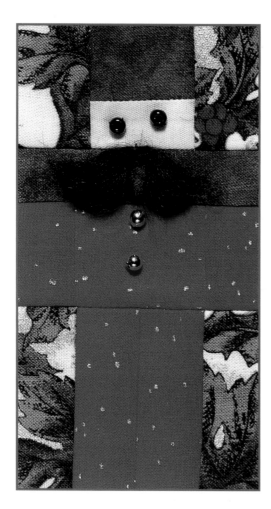

# Nutcracker

*Finished Size:* 2" x 4"

*Difficulty Level:* Moderate

*Joining Sequence:*

A + B = AB

AB + C = Nutcracker

*Details:*

EYES–Stitch ⅛"-diameter beads or buttons to face as indicated.

MUSTACHE–Stitch imitation hair to the bottom of the face section.

BUTTONS–Stitch ⅛"-diameter gold beads to nutcracker as shown.

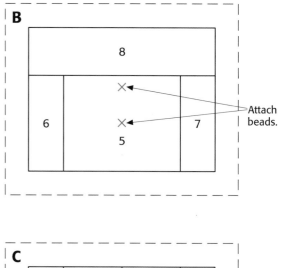

Attach beads.

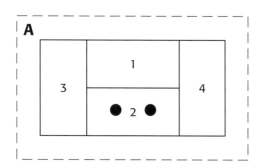

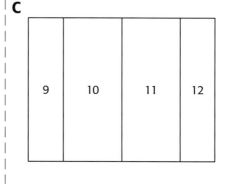

# $\mathcal{S}$nowman

*Finished Size:* 2" x 4"

*Difficulty Level:* Moderate

*Joining Sequence:*

A + B = AB

AB + C = Snowman

## *Details:*

EYES–Stitch ⅛"-diameter beads to face as indicated.

BUTTONS–Stitch ¼"-diameter buttons
to body as indicated.

SCARF–Stitch red scrap of fabric to body as indicated.

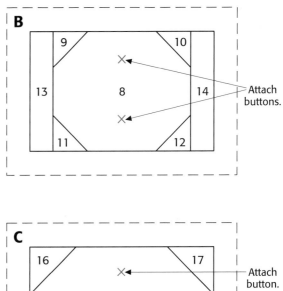

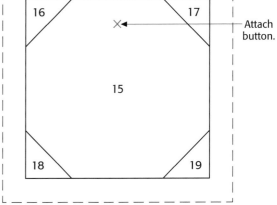

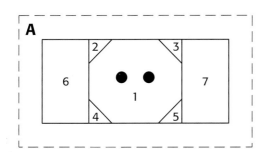

# Reindeer

*Finished Size:* 4" x 6"

*Difficulty Level:* Complex

*Joining Sequence:*

B + C = BC

A + BC = ABC

D + E = DE

DE + F = DEF

ABC + DEF = Reindeer

*Details:*

EYE—Stitch ⅛"-diameter bead or button to face as indicated.

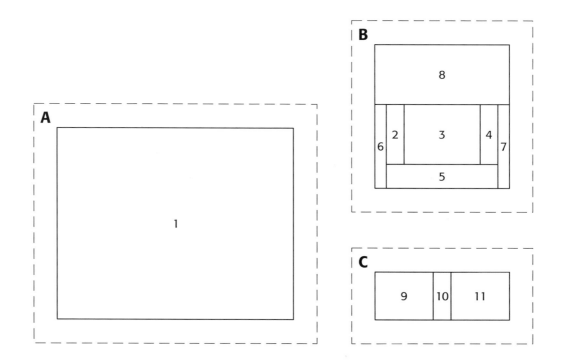

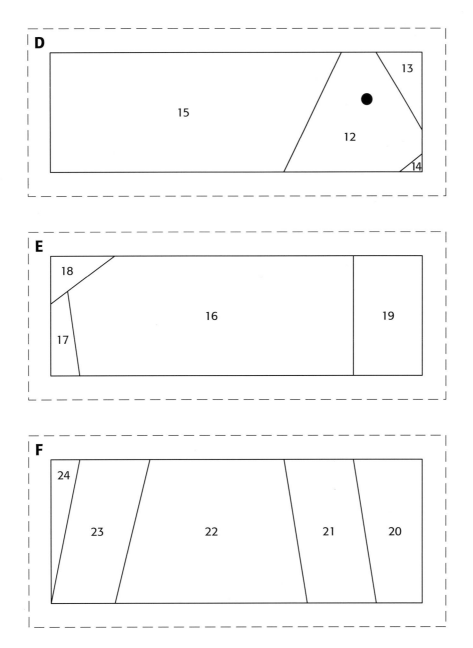

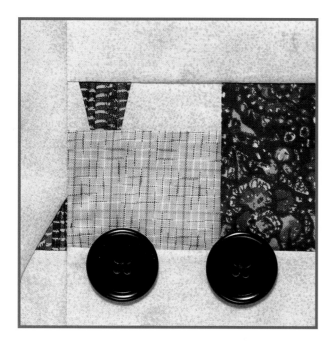

# *Train I—Engine*

*Finished Size:* 4" x 4"

*Difficulty Level:* Moderate

*Joining Sequence:*
A + B = Train I

*Details:*
WHEELS—Stitch ¾"- or 1"-diameter buttons to train
as indicated.

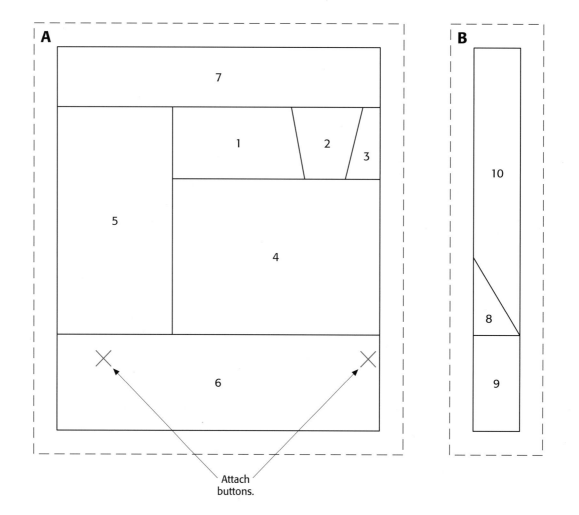

Attach
buttons.

# Train II—Passenger Car

*Finished Size:* 4" x 4"

*Difficulty Level:* Easy

*Details:*

WHEELS—Stitch ¾"-diameter buttons to train as indicated.

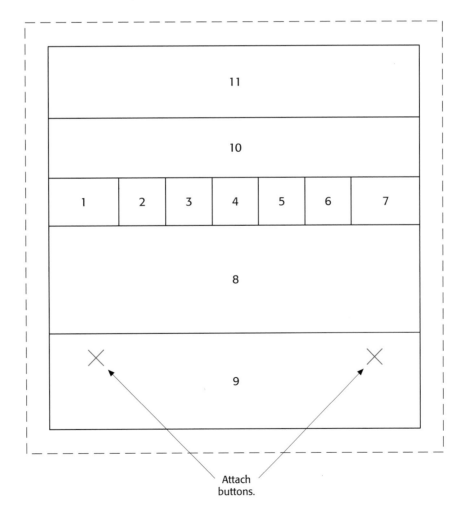

Attach buttons.

# Train III—Coal Car

*Finished Size:* 4" x 4"

*Difficulty Level:* Easy

*Details:*

WHEELS–Stitch ¾"-diameter buttons to train as indicated.

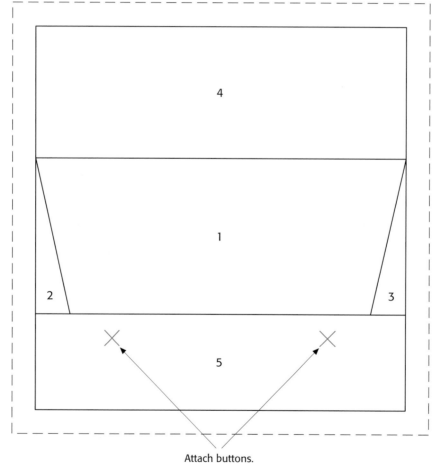

Attach buttons.

# Train IV—Caboose

*Finished Size:* 4" x 4"

*Difficulty Level:* Moderate

*Joining Sequence:*
A + B = Train IV

*Details:*
WHEELS—Stitch ¾"-diameter buttons to train as indicated.

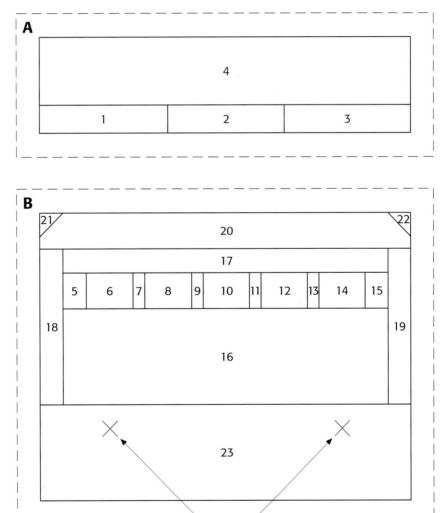

Attach buttons.

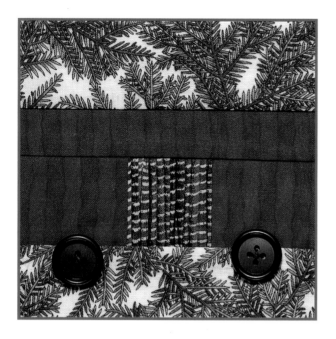

# Train V–Box Car

*Finished Size:* 4" x 4"

*Difficulty Level:* Easy

*Details:*

WHEELS–Stitch ¾"-diameter buttons to train
as indicated.

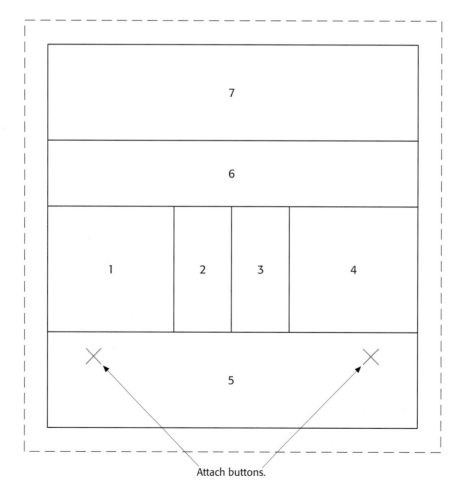

Attach buttons.

# Sleigh

*Finished Size:* 4" x 4"

*Difficulty Level:* Moderate

*Joining Sequence:*
A + B = Sleigh

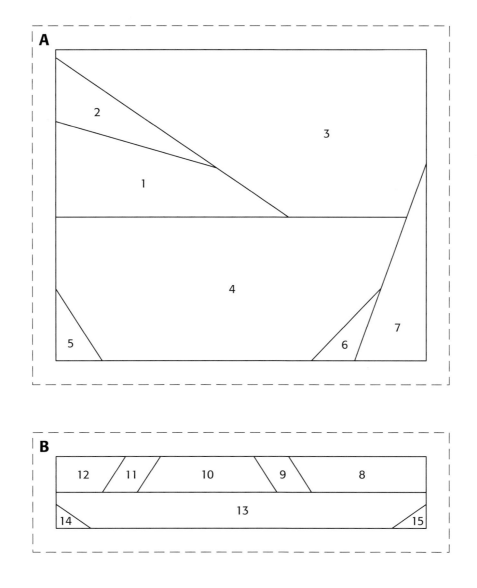

# Candle

*Finished Size:* 2" x 4"

*Difficulty Level:* Easy

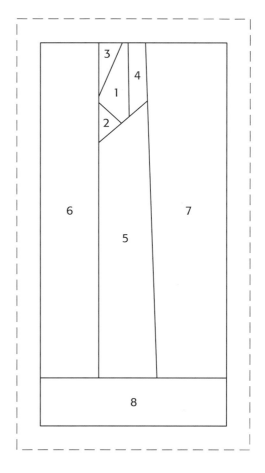

# Doll

*Finished Size:* 2" x 4"

*Difficulty Level:* Moderate

*Joining Sequence:*

A + B = AB

C + D = CD

CD + E = CDE

AB + CDE = Doll

*Details:*

EYES–Stitch ⅛"-diameter beads or buttons to face as indicated.

Bow–Stitch ¼"-wide ribbon under face as indicated.

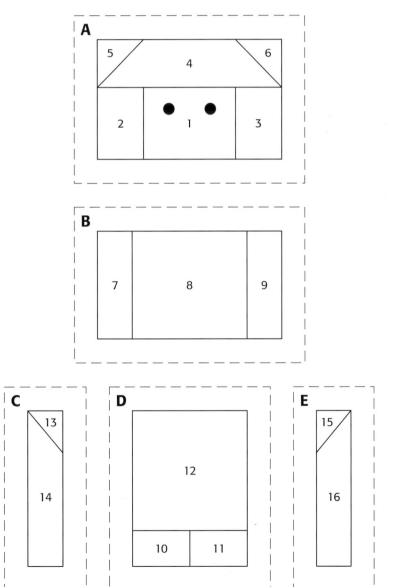

# Gingerbread Boy

*Finished Size:* 4" x 4"

*Difficulty Level:* Moderate

*Joining Sequence:*

A + B = Gingerbread Boy

*Details:*

EYES—Stitch ⅛"-diameter beads or buttons to face as indicated.

OUTLINE—Stitch ⅛"-wide white rickrack as indicated.

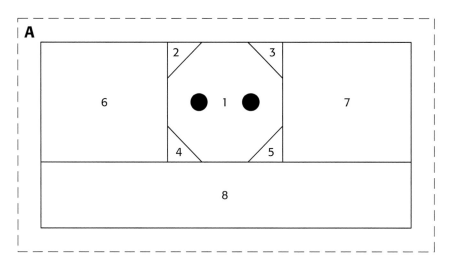

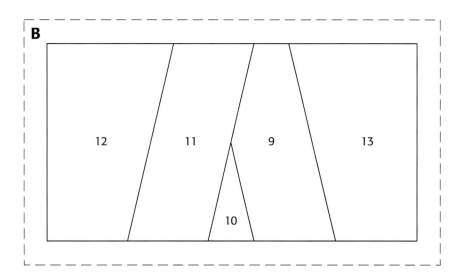

# Gingerbread Girl

*Finished Size:* 4" x 4"

*Difficulty Level:* Moderate

*Joining Sequence:*
A + B = Gingerbread Girl

*Details:*
EYES—Stitch ⅛"-diameter beads or buttons to face as indicated.

OUTLINE—Stitch ⅛"-wide white rickrack as indicated.

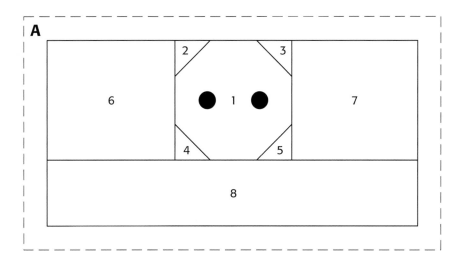

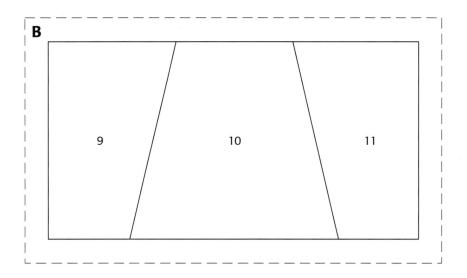

# $\mathcal{D}$ove

*Finished Size:* 4" x 4"

*Difficulty Level:* Moderate

*Joining Sequence:*
A + B = AB
AB + C = Dove

*Details:*
EYE—Stitch $\frac{1}{16}$"- or $\frac{1}{8}$"-diameter bead to head
as indicated.

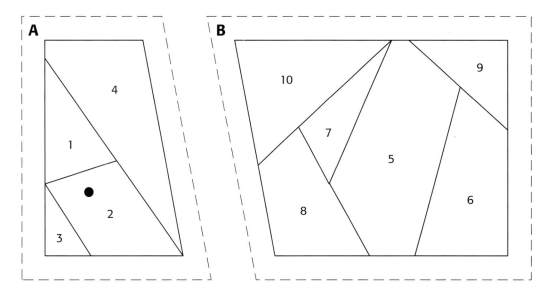

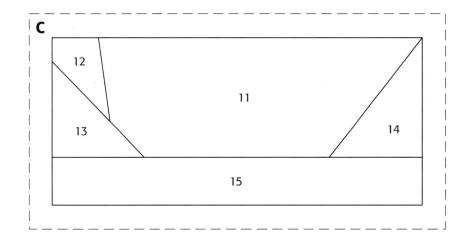

# Christmas Basket

*Finished Size:* 4" x 4"

*Difficulty Level:* Moderate

*Joining Sequence:*

A + B = Christmas Basket

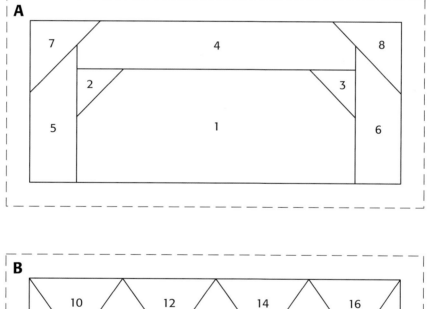

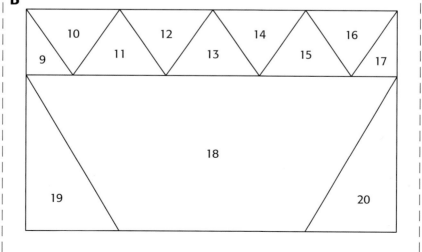

# Angel

---

*Finished Size:* 6" x 6"

*Difficulty Level:* Moderate

*Joining Sequence:*

B + C = BC

A + BC = Angel

*Details:*

EYE–Stitch $^1/_{16}$"-diameter bead to face as indicated.

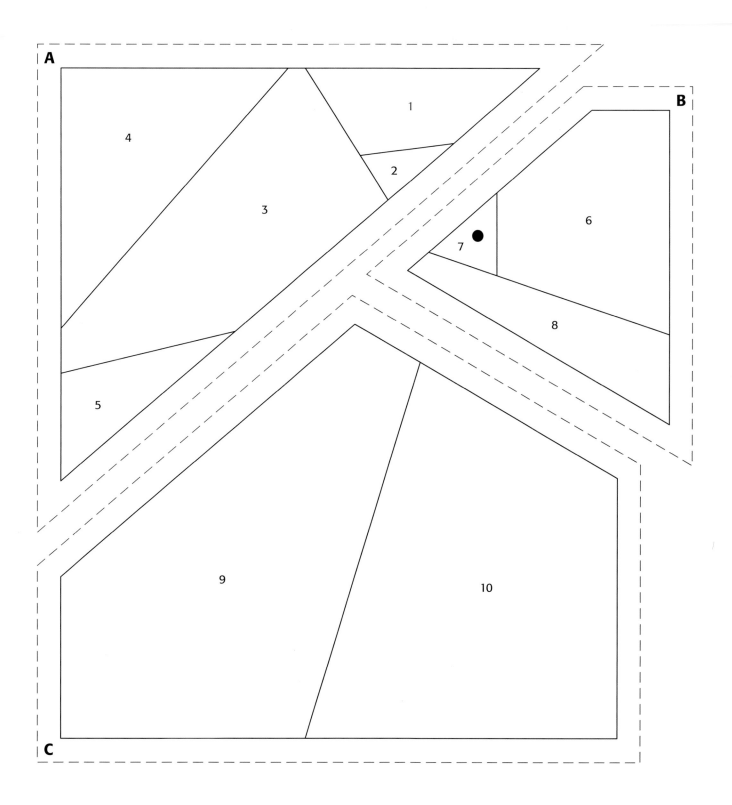

# Christmas Rose

*Finished Size:* 4" x 4"

*Difficulty Level:* Easy

*Joining Sequence:*
A + B = AB
C + D = CD
AB + CD = Christmas Rose

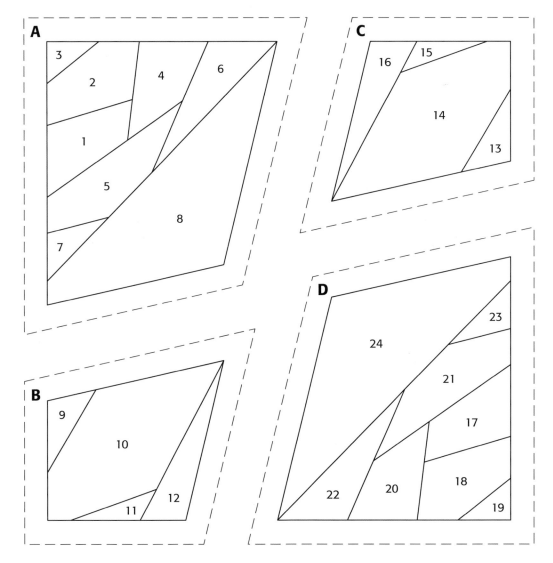

# Christmas Cactus

*Finished Size:* 4" x 4"

*Difficulty Level:* Easy

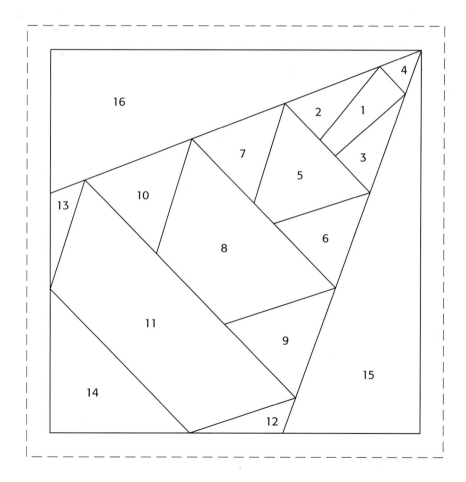

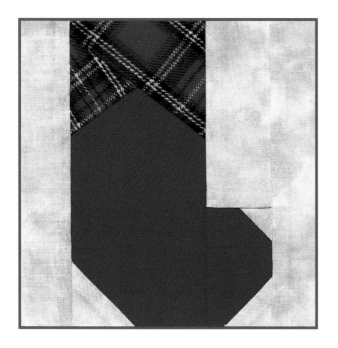

# Stocking I

*Finished Size:* 4" x 4"

*Difficulty Level:* Moderate

*Joining Sequence:*
A + B = Stocking I

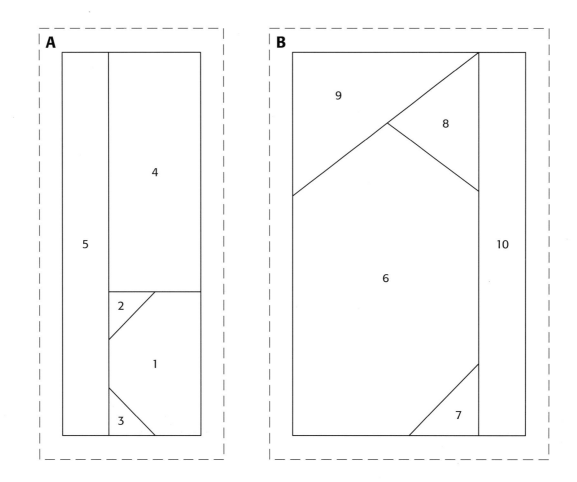

# Stocking II

*Finished Size:* 4" x 4"

*Difficulty Level:* Moderate

*Joining Sequence:*
A + B = Stocking II

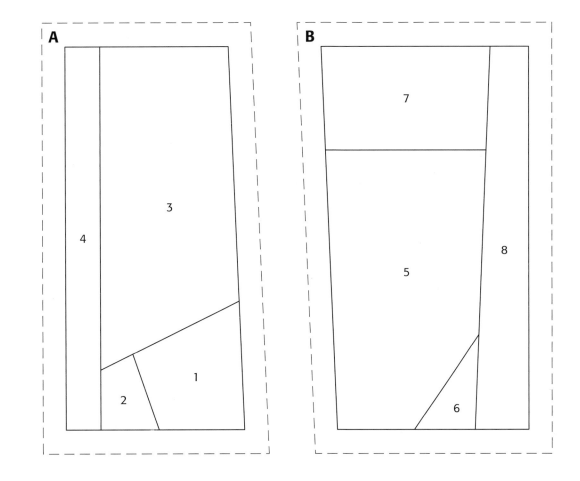

# Stocking III

*Finished Size:* 4" x 4"

*Difficulty Level:* Moderate

*Joining Sequence:*
A + B = Stocking III

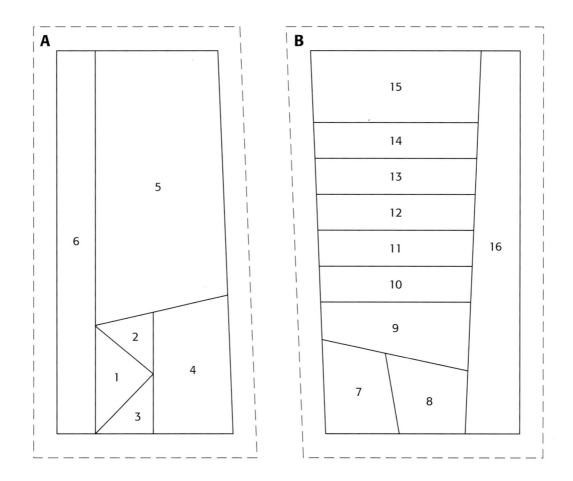

# Ribbon Border

*Finished Size:* 1" x 6"

*Difficulty Level:* Easy

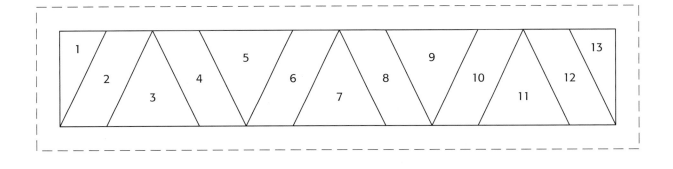

# Candy-Striped Border

*Border Finished Size:* 2" x 4"

*Corner Finished Size:* 2" x 2"

*Difficulty Level:* Easy

*Joining Sequence for Border Corner:*
A + B = Candy-Striped Border Corner

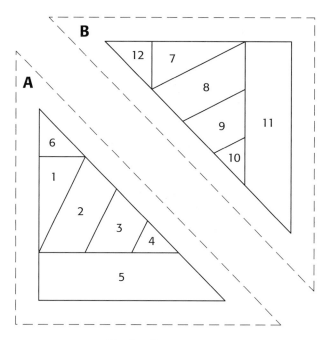

**Border Corner**

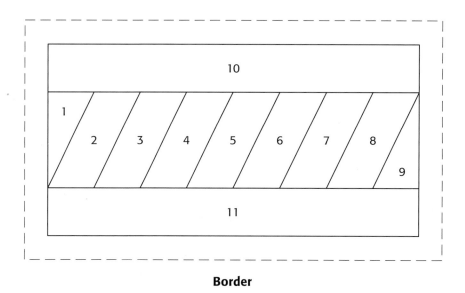

**Border**

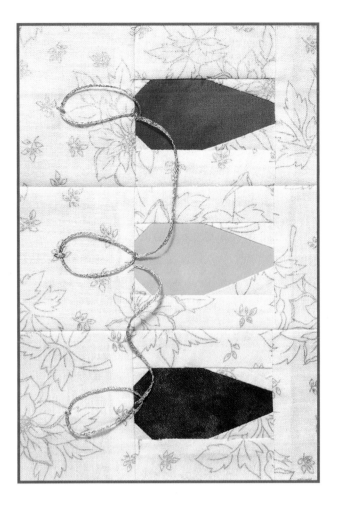

# Christmas Light Border

*Finished Size:* 2" x 4"

*Difficulty Level:* Easy

*Details:*

Cord–Stitch gold ribbon to blocks as indicated.

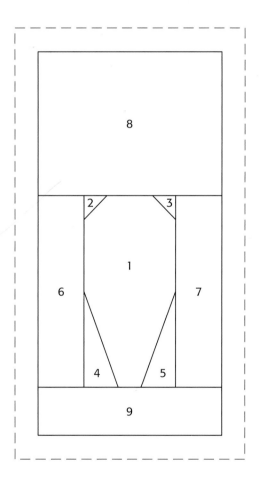

# Santa Hat Border

*Finished Size:* 2" x 4"

*Difficulty Level:* Easy

*Details:*

HAT—Stitch ¼"-diameter pompon to hat tips
as indicated.

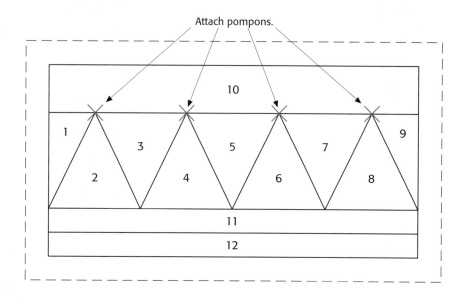

QUILTS

# ✣ CHRISTMAS ROSE ✣

CHRISTMAS ROSE *by Jodie Davis, 1998, Canton, Georgia, 24½" x 24½". Pieced and quilted by Kathy Semone.*

## Materials

*42"-wide fabric*

* ⅛ yd. *each* of 6 assorted red prints
* ⅛ yd. *each* of 6 assorted green prints
* ¼ yd. white solid for inner border
* ½ yd. red print for outer border
* 30" x 30" square of batting
* 1 yd. fabric for backing
* ¼ yd. green print for binding

## Cutting

**From the inner border fabric, cut:**

2 strips, each 1½" x 42". Crosscut the strips to make:
* 2 strips, each 1½" x 16½", for the inner side borders
* 2 strips, each 1½" x 18½", for the inner top and bottom borders

**From the outer border fabric, cut:**

3 strips, each 3½" x 42". Crosscut the strips to make:
* 2 strips, each 3½" x 18½", for the outer side borders
* 2 strips, each 3½" x 24½", for the outer top and bottom borders

**From the backing fabric, cut:**

1 square, 30" x 30"

## Quilt Top Assembly

1. Refer to "Transferring the Patterns" on pages 5–6 to prepare 16 foundations of the Christmas Rose pattern on page 52.

2. To piece each block, refer to "Basic Paper Piecing" on pages 7–8 and the instructions in "Joining Sequence" that appears on the same page as the pattern.

3. Arrange the blocks into 4 rows of 4 blocks each as shown.

4. Stitch the blocks together into rows. Remove the paper from the stitched seam allowances. Press the seam allowances open. Stitch the rows together. Remove the paper from the stitched seam allowances. Press the seam allowances open.

5. Stitch the inner side border strips to the quilt. Press the seam allowances toward the border strips. Stitch the inner top and bottom border strips to the quilt. Press the seam allowances toward the border strips.

6. Remove any remaining paper foundations.

7. Stitch the outer side border strips to the quilt. Press the seam allowances toward the border strips. Stitch the outer border top and bottom strips to the top and bottom edge of the quilt. Press the seam allowances toward the border strips.

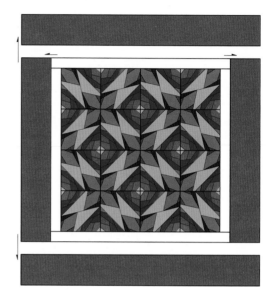

8. Following the instructions in "Preparing for Quilting" on page 11, layer the quilt top with batting and backing.

9. Quilt as desired.

10. Refer to "Making and Applying Binding" on pages 11–14 to make the binding and bind the quilt edges. Use the binding method of your choice.

# ➤➤ REINDEER EXPRESS ➤➤

REINDEER EXPRESS *by Jodie Davis, 1998, Canton, Georgia, 22½" x 14½". Pieced and quilted by Kathy Semone.*

## Materials

*42"-wide fabric*

* ¼ yd. medium brown print for reindeer bodies
* 4" x 4" square of dark brown print for reindeer antlers
* ½ yd. medium blue print for block backgrounds
* 6" x 6" square of brown-and-red plaid for sleigh
* 1½" x 9" strip of black solid for sleigh runners
* ⅛ yd. light blue print for inner border
* ¼ yd. holly print for outer border
* 20" x 32" piece of batting
* ¾ yd. fabric for backing
* ¼ yd. dark blue print for binding
* 3 black buttons or beads, ⅛" diameter, for reindeer eyes
* 1 yd. of ⅛"-wide gold metallic ribbon for harness
* 9 bells, ¼" diameter, for harness
* 1 red ball button, ½" diameter, for Rudolph's nose
* Assorted miniature toys to fill sleigh

## Cutting

**From the block background fabric, cut:**
1 rectangle, 2½" x 4½"

**From the inner border fabric, cut:**
2 strips, each 1" x 42". Crosscut the strips to make:
  * 2 strips, each 1" x 6½", for the inner side borders
  * 2 strips, each 1" x 17½", for the inner top and bottom borders

**From the outer border fabric, cut:**
2 strips, each 3" x 42". Crosscut the strips to make:
  * 2 strips, each 3" x 7½", for the outer side borders
  * 2 strips, each 3" x 22½", for the outer top and bottom borders

**From the backing fabric, cut:**
1 rectangle, 20" x 32"

## Quilt Top Assembly

1. Refer to "Transferring the Patterns" on pages 5–6 to prepare 3 foundations of the Reindeer pattern on page 36 and 1 foundation of the Sleigh pattern on page 43.

2. To piece each block, refer to "Basic Paper Piecing" on pages 7–8 and the instructions in "Joining Sequence" that appears on the same page as the patterns.

3. Stitch the 2½" x 4½" background rectangle to the top of the Sleigh block.

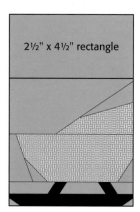

2½" x 4½" rectangle

4. Stitch the blocks together horizontally as shown. Remove the paper from the stitched seam allowances. Press the seam allowances open.

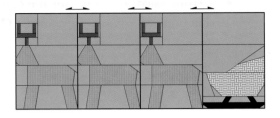

5. Stitch the inner side border strips to the quilt. Press the seam allowances toward the border strips. Stitch the inner top and bottom border strips to the quilt. Press the seam allowances toward the border strips.

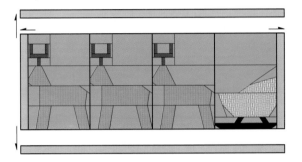

6. Remove any remaining paper foundations.

7. Stitch the outer side border strips to the quilt. Press the seam allowances toward the border strips. Stitch the outer top and bottom border strips to the quilt. Press the seam allowances toward the border strips.

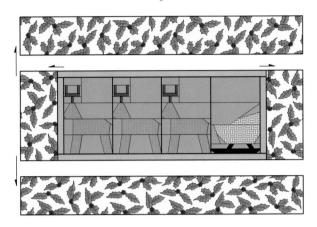

8. Following the instructions in "Preparing for Quilting" on page 11, layer the quilt top with batting and backing.

9. Quilt as desired.

10. Refer to "Making and Applying Binding" on pages 11–14 to make the binding and bind the quilt edges. Use the binding method of your choice.

11. Arrange the miniature toys on the Sleigh block as desired. Stitch them in place. Stitch the buttons, gold ribbon, small bells, and Rudolph's red-button nose to the quilt, as indicated in the quilt photo.

# ➤➤➤ *TRIM THE TREES* ⧫⧫⧫

TRIM THE TREES *by Jodie Davis, 1999, Canton, Georgia, 14½" x 24½". Pieced and quilted by Kathy Semone.*

## Materials

*42"-wide fabric*

* ✳ 2" x 18" strip *each* of 7 assorted green prints for trees
* ✳ ¼ yd. blue print for Christmas Tree I, II, and III block backgrounds
* ✳ ¼ yd. green print for inserted border and binding
* ✳ 2" x 3" piece *each* of 22 assorted prints for Christmas Light Border blocks
* ✳ ¼ yd. gold print for Christmas Star blocks
* ✳ ¾ yd. green print for Christmas Star and Christmas Light Border block backgrounds
* ✳ 20" x 30" piece of batting
* ✳ ¾ yd. fabric for backing
* ✳ 3 star buttons, 1" diameter, for Christmas Tree blocks
* ✳ 2½ yds. gold metallic cord for Christmas Light Border blocks

## Cutting

**From the Christmas Tree I, II, and III block background fabric, cut:**

2 strips, each 1½" x 42". Crosscut the strips to make:
* • 6 strips, each 1½" x 4½", for the vertical sashing
* • 4 strips, each 1½" x 6½", for the horizontal sashing

**From the inserted border fabric, cut:**

2 strips, each 1¼" x 42". Crosscut the strips to make:
* • 2 strips, each 1¼" x 16½", for the inserted side borders
* • 2 strips, each 1¼" x 6½", for the inserted top and bottom borders

**From the backing fabric, cut:**

1 rectangle, 20" x 30"

## Quilt Top Assembly

1. Refer to "Transferring the Patterns" on pages 5–6 to prepare 1 foundation each of the Christmas Tree I, Christmas Tree II, and Christmas Tree III patterns on pages 24–26; 4 foundations of the Christmas Star pattern on page 29; and 22 foundations of the Christmas Light Border pattern on page 59.

2. To piece each block, refer to "Basic Paper Piecing" on pages 7–8. To assemble the Christmas Star block, follow the instructions in "Joining Sequence" that appears on the same page as the pattern.

3. Stitch a vertical sashing strip to each side of the Christmas Tree blocks. Remove the paper from the stitched seam allowances. Press the seam allowances toward the sashing.

4. Arrange the 3 blocks vertically as desired. Alternately stitch the horizontal sashing strips and blocks together, beginning and ending with a sashing strip. Remove the paper from the stitched seam allowances. Press the seam allowances toward the sashing.

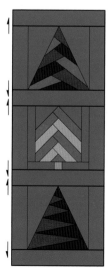

5. Press the inserted side border strips in half lengthwise, wrong sides together. With the sashing and inserted side border raw edges even, baste the inserted border strips to the quilt sides ¼" from the raw edges. Repeat for the inserted top and bottom border strips.

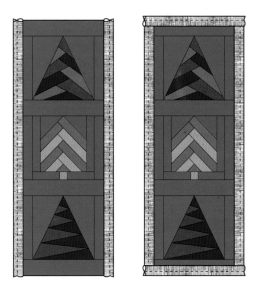

6. To make the outer side borders, stitch together 8 Christmas Light Border blocks. Make 2 borders. Remove the paper from the stitched seam allowances. Press the seam allowances open.

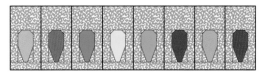

Outer side borders
Make 2.

7. To make the outer top and bottom borders, stitch together 3 Christmas Light Border blocks. Stitch a Christmas Star block to each end of the strip. Make 2 borders. Remove the paper from the stitched seam allowances. Press the seam allowances open.

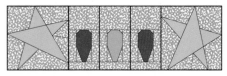

Outer top and bottom borders
Make 2.

8. Stitch the outer side borders to the quilt. Remove the paper from the stitched seam allowances. Press the seam allowances toward the outer border strips. Stitch the outer top and bottom borders to the quilt. Remove the paper from the stitched seam allowances. Press the seam allowances toward the outer border strips.

9. Remove any remaining paper foundations.

10. Following the instructions in "Preparing for Quilting" on page 11, layer the quilt top with batting and backing.

11. Quilt as desired.

12. Refer to "Making and Applying Binding" on pages 11–14 to make the binding and bind the quilt edges. Use the binding method of your choice.

13. Stitch a star button to the top of each tree. Refer to the photo to stitch the gold cord to the outer border. Tack the cord at the base of each light bulb and at the center of the *U* that forms between each light bulb.

CHRISTMAS CACTUS *by Jodie Davis, 1998, Canton, Georgia, 26½" x 34½". Pieced and quilted by Kathy Semone.*

## Materials

*42"-wide fabric*

* ½ yd. multicolor print for cactus
* ¾ yd. off-white solid for background
* ¾ yd. blue print for border
* 32" x 40" piece of batting
* 1⅛ yds. fabric for backing
* ¼ yd. red print for binding

## Cutting

**From the multicolor print, cut:**
   2" x 42" strips

**From the border fabric, cut:**
   4 strips, each 5½" x 42". Crosscut the strips to make:
   • 2 strips, each 5½" x 24½", for the side borders
   • 2 strips, each 5½" x 34½", for the top and bottom borders

**From the backing fabric, cut:**
   1 rectangle, 32" x 40"

## Quilt Top Assembly

1. Refer to "Transferring the Patterns" on pages 5–6 to prepare 24 foundations of the Christmas Cactus pattern on page 53.

2. Refer to "Basic Paper Piecing" on pages 7–8 to piece each block with the multicolor print 2" strips and off-white solid fabric.

3. Arrange the blocks into 6 rows of 4 blocks each as shown.

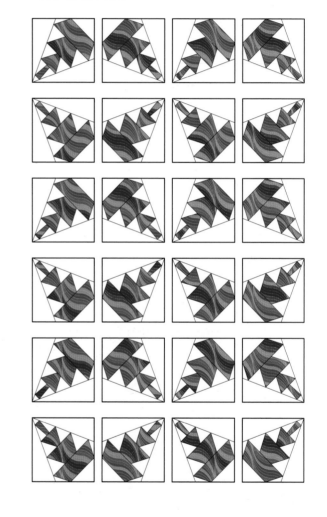

4. Stitch the blocks together into rows. Remove the paper from the stitched seam allowances. Press the seam allowances open. Stitch the rows together. Remove the paper from the stitched seam allowances. Press the seam allowances open.

5. Stitch the side border strips to the quilt. Remove the paper from the stitched seam allowances. Press the seam allowances toward the border strips. Stitch the top and bottom border strips to the quilt. Remove the paper from the stitched seam allowances. Press the seam allowances toward the border strips.

6. Remove any remaining paper foundations.

7. Following the instructions in "Preparing for Quilting" on page 11, layer the quilt top with batting and backing.

8. Quilt as desired.

9. Refer to "Making and Applying Binding" on pages 11–14 to make the binding and bind the quilt edges. Use the binding method of your choice.

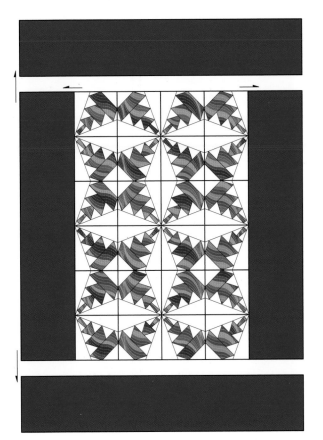

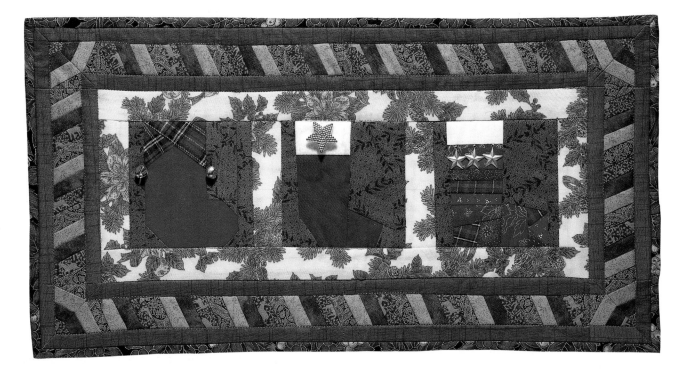

THE STOCKINGS WERE HUNG *by Jodie Davis, 1998, Canton, Georgia, 20½" x 10½". Pieced and quilted by Kathy Semone.*

## Materials

*42"-wide fabric*

* 7 assorted red prints: 6" x 6" square or larger of 2 prints for Stocking I and II blocks; scraps of 5 prints for Stocking III block
* Scrap of red plaid for top of Stocking I block
* Scraps of 2 white prints for tops of Stocking II and III blocks
* 6 assorted brown prints: ¼ yd. of 1 print for block background; ⅛ yd. *each* of 5 prints for Candy-Striped Border blocks
* ¼ yd. cream print for sashing
* 16" x 26" piece of batting
* ⅝ yd. fabric for backing
* ¼ yd. holly print for binding
* 2 gold jingle bells, ⅜" diameter, for Stocking I block
* 1 gold star button, 1" diameter, for Stocking II block
* 3 gold star buttons, ⅝" diameter, for Stocking III block

## Cutting

**From the sashing fabric, cut:**
2 strips, each 1½" x 42". Crosscut the strips to make:
* 4 strips, each 1½" x 4½", for the vertical sashing
* 2 strips, each 1½" x 16½", for the horizontal sashing

**From the backing fabric, cut:**
1 rectangle, 16" x 26"

## Quilt Top Assembly

1. Refer to "Transferring the Patterns" on pages 5–6 to prepare 1 foundation each of the Stocking I, II, and III patterns on pages 54–56; 4 foundations of the Candy-Striped Border Corner pattern on page 58; and 4 foundations of the Candy-Striped Border pattern on page 58—2 with a finished length of 6" for the side borders and 2 with a finished length of 20" for the top and bottom borders.

2. To piece each block and border section, refer to "Basic Paper Piecing" on pages 7–8. To assemble the Candy-Striped Border Corner pattern, follow the instructions in "Joining Sequence" on the same page as the pattern.

3. Arrange the 3 Stocking blocks horizontally as desired. Alternately stitch the vertical sashing strips and blocks together, beginning and ending with a sashing strip. Remove the paper from the stitched seam allowances. Press the seam allowances toward the sashing.

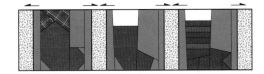

4. Stitch the horizontal sashing strips to the top and bottom edges of the block unit. Remove the paper from the stitched seam allowances. Press the seam allowances toward the sashing.

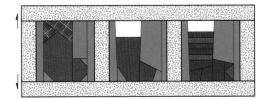

5. Stitch the side border strips to the quilt. Remove the paper from the stitched seam allowances. Press the seam allowances open.

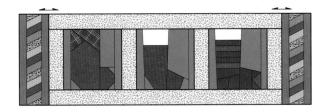

6. Stitch a Candy-Striped Border Corner block to each end of the top and bottom border strips as shown. Remove the paper from the stitched seam allowances. Press the seam allowances open. Stitch the strips to the top and bottom edges of the quilt. Remove the paper from the stitched seam allowances. Press the seam allowances open.

Make 2.

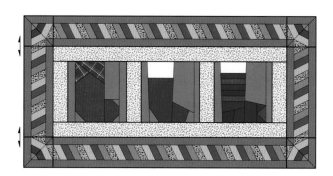

7. Remove any remaining paper foundations.

8. Following the instructions in "Preparing for Quilting" on page 11, layer the quilt top with batting and backing.

9. Quilt as desired.

10. Refer to "Making and Applying Binding" on pages 11–14 to make the binding and bind the quilt edges. Use the mitered corner method.

11. Refer to the quilt photo to stitch the bells and buttons to the cuffs of each Stocking block.

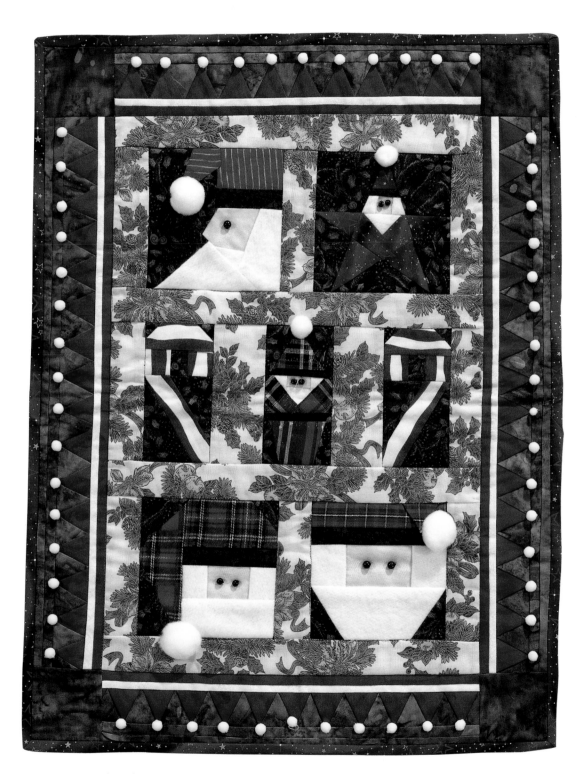

S<small>ANTA</small>! *by Jodie Davis, 1998, Canton, Georgia, 15½" x 20½". Pieced and quilted by Kathy Semone.*

## Materials

*42"-wide fabric*

* Scraps of assorted white prints, black prints, red prints, and solid in any skin color for Santa I, II, III, IV, and V blocks
* 2" x 22" strip of red-and-white striped print for Candy Cane blocks
* ⅛ yd. dark green print for block backgrounds
* ¼ yd. red solid for border
* ⅛ yd. white solid for border
* ¼ yd. green print for border
* ⅜ yd. cream print for sashing
* 21" x 26" piece of batting
* ¾ yd. fabric for backing
* ⅛ yd. red print for binding
* 2 white pompons, 1" diameter, for Santa I, Santa IV, and Santa V blocks
* 2 white pompons, ½" diameter, for Santa II and Santa III blocks
* 54 white pompons, ¼" diameter, for Santa Hat Border blocks
* 6 buttons or beads, ⅛" diameter, for Santa II, Santa III, and Santa IV blocks
* 3 buttons, ¼" diameter, for Santa I and Santa V blocks

## Cutting

**From the sashing fabric, cut:**

3 strips, each 1½" x 42". Crosscut the strips to make:
  * 8 strips, each 1½" x 4½", for vertical sashing
  * 4 strips, each 1½" x 11½", for horizontal sashing

1 strip, 2" x 42". Crosscut the strip to make:
  * 2 strips, each 2" x 4½", for vertical sashing

**From the green print, cut:**

4 squares, each 2½" x 2½", for the border corner blocks

**From the backing fabric, cut:**

1 rectangle, 21" x 26"

## Quilt Top Assembly

1. Refer to "Transferring the Patterns" on pages 5–6 to prepare 1 foundation each of the Santa I, II, III, IV, and V patterns on pages 15–19; 2 foundations of the Candy Cane pattern on page 23—1 pattern should be a mirror image; and 4 foundations of the Santa Hat Border pattern on page 60—2 patterns with a finished length of 6" for the side borders and 2 patterns with a finished length of 16" for the top and bottom borders.

2. To piece each block and border section, refer to "Basic Paper Piecing" on pages 7–8 and follow the instructions in "Joining Sequence" that appears on the same page as the patterns.

3. Assemble and then stitch the blocks and the appropriate vertical sashing strips into rows as shown. Remove the paper from the stitched seam allowances. Press the seam allowances toward the sashing.

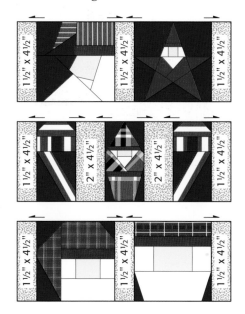

4. Arrange the 3 rows vertically as shown. Alternately stitch the horizontal sashing strips and rows together, beginning and ending with a sashing strip. Remove the paper from the stitched seam allowances. Press the seam allowances toward the sashing.

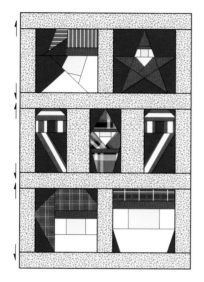

5. Stitch the side border strips to the quilt. Remove the paper from the stitched seam allowances. Press the seam allowances open.

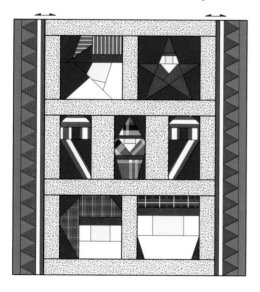

6. Stitch a 2½" border corner block to each end of the top and bottom border strips. Remove the paper from the stitched seam allowances. Press the seam allowances toward the corner blocks. Stitch the border strips to the top and bottom edges of the quilt. Remove the paper from the stitched seam allowances. Press the seam allowances open.

Make 2.

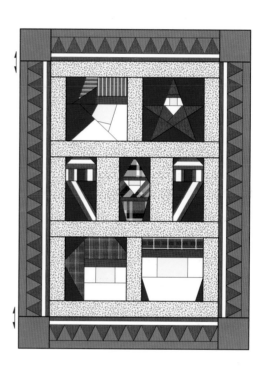

7. Remove any remaining paper foundations.

8. Following the instructions in "Preparing for Quilting" on page 11, layer the quilt top with batting and backing.

9. Quilt as desired.

10. Refer to "Making and Applying Binding" on pages 11–14 to make the binding and bind the quilt edges. Use the binding method of your choice.

11. Stitch the pompons to the Santa hat tips. Stitch the buttons or beads to each Santa block as indicated in the block patterns on pages 15–19.

# GINGERBREAD CELEBRATION

GINGERBREAD CELEBRATION *by Jodie Davis, 1998, Canton, Georgia, 22½" x 14½". Pieced and quilted by Kathy Semone.*

## Materials

*42"-wide fabric*

* ⅛ yd. brown print for Gingerbread Boy and Girl blocks
* ¼ yd. cream print for block backgrounds and Candy-Striped Border blocks
* ⅛ yd. red-and-white striped print for Candy Cane blocks
* ⅛ yd. red print for Candy-Striped Border blocks
* ⅛ yd. blue print for Candy-Striped Border blocks
* ⅜ yd. green print for outer border
* 20" x 28" piece of batting
* ¾ yd. fabric for backing
* ⅛ yd. red print for binding
* 1 yd. of ⅝"-wide red satin ribbon
* 4 black beads or buttons, ⅛" diameter, for eyes
* 1 package of ⅛"-wide white rickrack

## Cutting

**From the outer border fabric, cut:**

2 strips, each 3½" x 42". Crosscut the strips to make:
* 2 strips, each 3½" x 8½", for the outer side borders
* 2 strips, each 3½" x 22½", for the outer top and bottom borders

**From the backing fabric, cut:**

1 rectangle, 20" x 28"

## Quilt Top Assembly

1. Refer to "Transferring the Patterns" on pages 5–6 to prepare 1 foundation of the Gingerbread Boy pattern on page 46; 1 foundation of the Gingerbread Girl pattern on page 47; 4 foundations of the Candy Cane pattern on page 23—2 patterns should be mirror images; and 2 foundations of the Candy-Striped Border pattern on page 58—each with a finished length of 16".

2. To piece each block and border section, refer to "Basic Paper Piecing" on pages 7–8 and follow the instructions in "Joining Sequence" that appears on the same page as the patterns.

3. Arrange the blocks horizontally as shown and stitch the blocks together. Remove the paper from the stitched seam allowances. Press the seam allowances open.

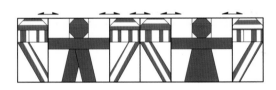

4. Stitch the Candy-Striped Border strips to the top and bottom of the block unit. Remove the paper from the stitched seam allowances. Press the seam allowances open.

5. Stitch the outer side border strips to the quilt. Remove the paper from the stitched seam allowances. Press the seam allowances toward the border strips. Stitch the outer top and bottom border strips to the quilt. Remove the paper from the stitched seam allowances. Press the seam allowances toward the border strips.

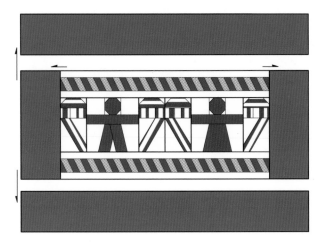

6. Remove any remaining paper foundations.

7. Following the instructions in "Preparing for Quilting" on page 11, layer the quilt top with batting and backing.

8. Quilt as desired.

9. Refer to "Making and Applying Binding" on pages 11–14 to make the binding and bind the quilt edges. Use the binding method of your choice.

10. Cut the red ribbon into 3 equal lengths. Tie each length into a bow. Tack 1 bow to each Candy Cane block. Stitch the black beads or buttons and rickrack to the Gingerbread Boy and Girl blocks as indicated in the block patterns on pages 46 and 47.

# CHRISTMAS MORNING SAMPLER

CHRISTMAS MORNING SAMPLER *by Jodie Davis, 1998, Canton, Georgia, 27½" x 21½". Pieced and quilted by Kathy Semone.*

## Materials

*42"-wide fabric*

* ¼ yd. red-and-white striped print for Candy Cane blocks
* Scraps of assorted fabrics for remaining blocks
* ½ yd. small green print for sashing, inner border, and binding
* ½ yd. large green print for outer border
* 27" x 33" piece of batting
* ⅞ yd. fabric for backing
* 5 black beads or buttons, ⅛" diameter, for eyes
* 10 black buttons, ¾" diameter, for train car wheels
* 10" piece of ¼"-wide green satin ribbon for Doll block
* Black imitation hair for beard in Nutcracker block and tail and mane in Rocking Horse block
* ¼ yd. of ⅛"-wide red satin ribbon for bridle in Rocking Horse block

## Cutting

**From the sashing, inner border, and binding fabric, cut:**

2 strips, each 1½" x 42". Crosscut the strips to make:
* 8 strips, each 1½" x 4½", for vertical sashing
* 2 strips, each 1½" x 20½", for horizontal sashing

2 strips, each 1" x 42". Crosscut the strips to make:
* 2 strips, each 1" x 14½", for the inner side borders
* 2 strips, each 1" x 21½", for the inner top and bottom borders

**From the outer border fabric, cut:**

3 strips, each 3½" x 42. Crosscut the strips to make:
* 72 strips, each 1½" x 3½", for the pieced side, top, and bottom outer borders
* 4 squares, each 3½" x 3½", for the outer border corner squares

**From the backing fabric, cut:**

1 rectangle, 27" x 33"

## Quilt Top Assembly

1. Refer to "Transferring the Patterns" on pages 5–6 to prepare 1 foundation each of the Train I (page 38), Train II (page 39), Train III (page 40), Train IV (page 41), Train V (page 42), Bow (page 32), Nutcracker (page 34), Doll (page 45), Rocking Horse (page 53), and Sled (page 30) patterns. Also prepare 8 foundations of the Candy Cane pattern on page 23—4 should be mirror images of the pattern.

2. Refer to "Basic Paper Piecing" on pages 7–8 to piece each block. Follow the instructions in "Joining Sequence" that appears on the same page as the patterns to assemble the blocks.

3. Stitch the Train blocks together as shown. Remove the paper from the stitched seam allowances. Press the seam allowances open.

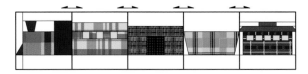

4. Stitch the remaining 2 rows together as shown, separating the blocks as indicated with a vertical sashing strip. Remove the paper from the stitched seam allowances. Press the seam allowances open.

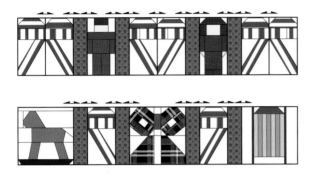

5. Stitch the 3 rows together in the sequence shown, separating each row with a horizontal sashing strip. Remove the paper from the stitched seam allowances. Press the seam allowances open.

6. Stitch the inner side border strips to the quilt. Remove the paper from the stitched seam allowances. Press the seam allowances toward the border strips. Stitch the inner top and bottom border strips to the quilt. Remove the paper from the stitched seam allowances. Press the seam allowances open.

7. To make the pieced outer side border strips, randomly stitch 15 of the 1½" x 3½" outer border strips together side by side. Make 2 borders. Stitch the outer border side strips to the quilt sides. Press the seam allowances open.

Make 2.

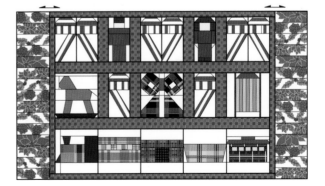

8. To make the pieced outer top and bottom border strips, randomly stitch 21 of the 1½" x 3½" outer border strips together side by side. Stitch an outer border corner square to each end of the pieced strip. Make 2 borders. Press the seam allowances open. Stitch the pieced outer top and bottom border strips to the quilt. Press the seam allowances open.

Make 2.

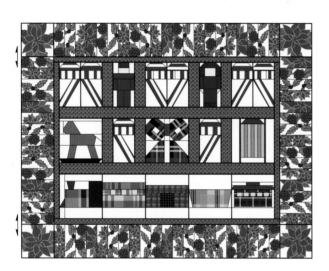

9. Remove any remaining paper foundations.

10. Following the instructions in "Preparing for Quilting" on page 11, layer the quilt top with batting and backing.

11. Quilt as desired.

12. Refer to "Making and Applying Binding" on pages 11–14 to make the binding and bind the quilt edges.

13. Stitch the ⅛"-diameter beads or buttons to the Nutcracker, Doll, and Rocking Horse blocks, and the ¾"-diameter buttons to the train cars as indicated on the patterns. Make a bow with the green satin ribbon and tack it to the Doll block below the face section. Stitch a small tuft of imitation hair to the Nutcracker block at the bottom of the face section and a larger tuft to the Rocking Horse block over the tail section. Refer to the photo to stitch the red satin ribbon to the Rocking Horse block for a bridle.

# RED BIRDS

RED BIRDS *by Jodie Davis, 1999, Canton, Georgia, 12½" x 8½". Pieced and quilted by Jodie Davis and Kathy Semone.*

## Materials

*42"-wide fabric*

* ⅛ yd. red solid for cardinal body
* Scrap of black solid for cardinal face
* ⅛ yd. green print for cardinal block background
* ⅛ yd. green print for holly
* ¼ yd. gold print for Holly block background and binding
* 14" x 18" piece of batting
* ½ yd. fabric for backing
* 2 black buttons, ⅛"-diameter, for eyes
* 8 red ball buttons, ½"-diameter, for berries
* Black, fine-tip permanent marker

## Quilt Top Assembly

1. Refer to "Transferring the Patterns" on pages 5–6 to prepare 2 foundations of the Cardinal pattern on page 22—1 should be a mirror image of the pattern; and 8 foundations of the Holly pattern on page 31.

2. To piece each Cardinal block, refer to "Basic Paper Piecing" on pages 7–8 and follow the instructions in "Joining Sequence" on the same page as the pattern.

3. Refer to "Paper Piecing Curved Seams" on page 9 to piece each Holly block.

4. Stitch the Cardinal blocks together with the birds facing each other. Remove the paper from the stitched seam allowance. Press the seam allowance open.

5. Stitch the Holly blocks together in pairs as shown. Make 4 pairs. Remove the paper from the stitched seam allowances. Press the seam allowances open.

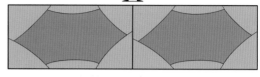

Make 4.

6. Stitch 1 pair of Holly blocks to the top of the Cardinal block unit. Repeat for the bottom. Remove the paper from the stitched seam allowances. Press the seam allowances open. Stitch 1 pair of Holly blocks to each of the quilt sides. Remove the paper from the stitched seam allowances. Press the seam allowances open.

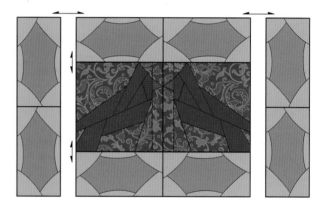

7. Remove any remaining paper foundations.

8. Following the instructions in "Preparing for Quilting" on page 11, layer the quilt top with batting and backing.

9. Quilt as desired.

10. Refer to "Making and Applying Binding" on pages 11–14 to make the binding and bind the quilt edges. Use the binding method of your choice.

11. Stitch the black buttons to the Cardinal blocks as indicated on the pattern. Referring to the photo for placement, stitch 2 red buttons to the center of each pair of Holly blocks. Draw in the birds' legs with the marker, if desired.

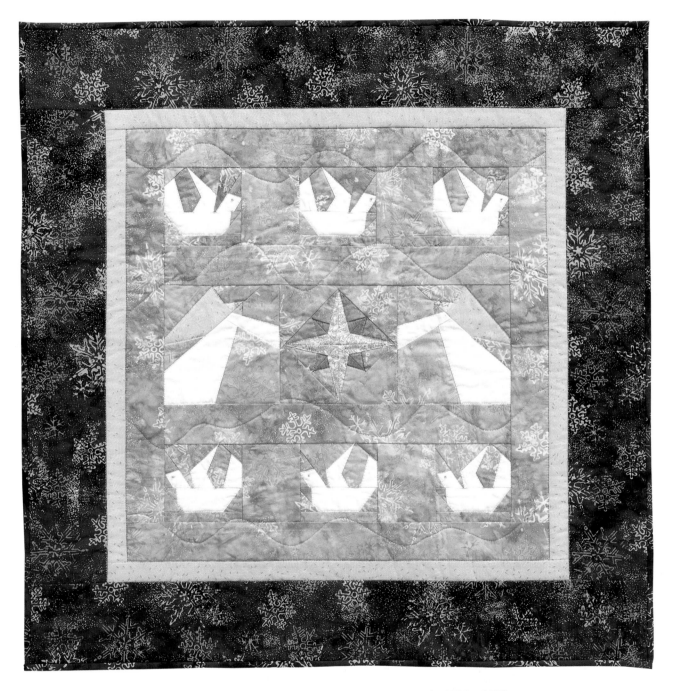

PEACE ON EARTH *by Jodie Davis, 1999, Canton, Georgia, 30½" x 30½".*

## Materials

*42"-wide fabric*

* ⅟₄ yd. white solid for angel dresses and doves
* ⅟₄ yd. yellow print for angel wings and middle border
* Scrap of light gold print for angel hair
* Scrap of solid in any skin color for angel face
* Scrap of medium gold print for star
* Scrap of dark gold print for star
* 1 yd. light blue print for block backgrounds, sashing, and inner border
* ¾ yd. dark blue print for outer border and binding
* 36" x 36" square of batting
* 1⅛ yds. fabric for backing
* 8 gold beads, ⅟₁₆" diameter, for dove and angel eyes

## Cutting

**From the background, sashing, and inner border fabric, cut:**

1 strip, 3½" x 42". Crosscut the strip to make:
* 4 strips, each 3½" x 4½", for the vertical sashing

2 strips, each 2½" x 42". Crosscut the strips to make:
* 4 strips, each 2½" x 18½", for the horizontal sashing and inner side borders
* 2 strips, each 2½" x 22½", for the inner top and bottom borders

2 squares, 4" x 4", for the Bright Star block extensions. Cut the squares in half diagonally to make:
* 4 half-square triangles

**From the middle border fabric, cut:**

4 strips, each 1½" x 42". Crosscut the strips to make:
* 2 strips, each 1½" x 22½", for the middle side borders
* 2 strips, each 1½" x 24½", for the middle top and bottom borders

**From the outer border fabric, cut:**

4 strips, each 3½" x 42". Crosscut the strips to make:
* 2 strips, each 3½" x 24½", for the outer side borders
* 2 strips, each 3½" x 30½", for the outer top and bottom borders

**From the backing fabric, cut:**

1 square, 36" x 36"

## Quilt Top Assembly

1. Refer to "Transferring the Patterns" on pages 5–6 to prepare 2 foundations of the Angel pattern on page 50—1 should be a mirror image of the pattern; 1 foundation of the Bright Star pattern on page 27; and 6 foundations of the Dove pattern on page 48—3 should be mirror images.

2. To piece each block, refer to "Basic Paper Piecing" on pages 7–8 and follow the instructions in "Joining Sequence" that appears on the same page as the patterns.

3. Stitch the cut edge of each half-square triangle to the edges of the Bright Star block. Remove the paper from the stitched seam allowances. Press the seam allowances open. Trim the block to measure 6½" x 6½".

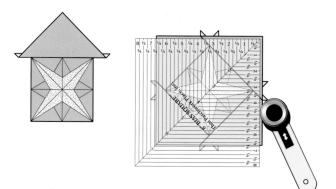

4. Stitch the Angel and Bright Star blocks together as shown. Remove the paper from the stitched seam allowances. Press the seam allowances open.

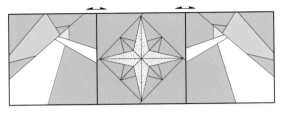

5. Stitch 3 Dove blocks and 2 vertical sashing strips together as shown. Make 2 rows, with all of the doves facing the same direction in each row. Remove the paper from the stitched seam allowances. Press the seam allowances open.

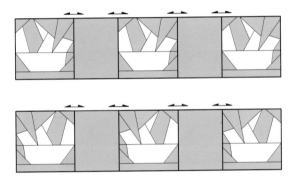

6. Stitch the Dove and Angel rows together as shown. Separate each row with a horizontal sashing strip. Remove the paper from the stitched seam allowances. Press the seam allowances open.

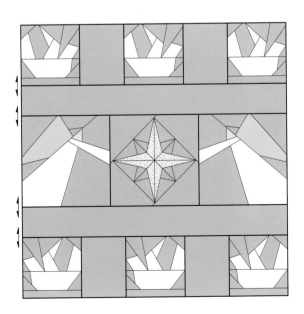

7. Stitch the inner side border strips to the quilt. Remove the paper from the stitched seam allowances. Press the seam allowances open. Stitch the inner top and bottom border strips to the quilt. Remove the paper from the stitched seam allowances. Press the seam allowances open.

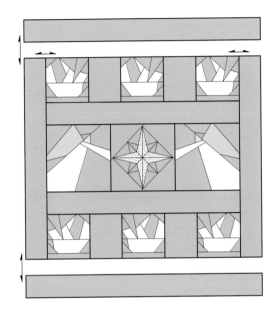

8. Remove any remaining paper foundations.

9. Stitch the middle side border strips to the quilt. Press the seam allowances toward the middle border strips. Stitch the middle top and bottom border strips to the quilt. Press the seam allowances toward the middle border.

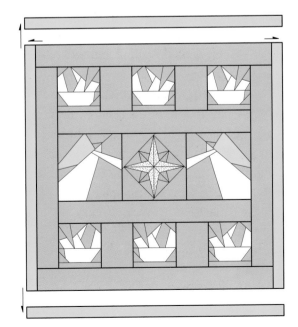

10. Stitch the outer side border strips to the quilt. Press the seam allowances toward the outer border strips. Stitch the outer top and bottom border strips to the quilt. Press the seam allowances toward the outer border strips.

11. Following the instructions in "Preparing for Quilting" on page 11, layer the quilt top with batting and backing.

12. Quilt as desired.

13. Refer to "Making and Applying Binding" on pages 11–14 to make the binding and bind the quilt edges.

14. Stitch the gold beads to the Dove and Angel blocks as indicated in the block patterns on pages 48 and 50.

# CHRISTMAS ORNAMENTS

Turn your blocks into package decorations or adorable ornaments for your Christmas tree. They are so quick and easy to whip up, you'll want to make extra for holiday giving. All you need in addition to the pieced block is an extra piece of backing fabric, a small amount of fiberfill, and a 12" length of ribbon.

## Instructions

1. Cut a piece of backing fabric the same size as the pieced block. Cut the ribbon in half widthwise.

2. Fold one length of ribbon in half to make a loop. Position the ribbon loop on the right side of the pieced block, aligning the raw edges at the center of the block upper edge. Place the backing fabric over the pieced block, right sides together. Stitch the block and backing together, leaving a 2"-wide opening at the bottom edge. Backstitch at the beginning and ending of the stitching.

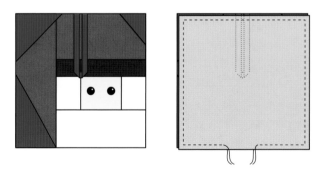

3. Trim the seam allowances at the corners.

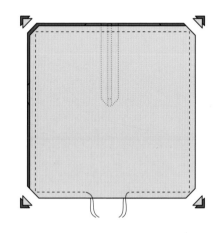

4. Turn the ornament right side out. If desired, stuff the ornament with fiberfill. Whipstitch the opening closed.

5. Tie the remaining ribbon length into a bow. Tack the bow to the top of the ornament at the base of the ribbon loop.

# RESOURCES

Nothing beats visiting a quilt shop to see all the latest sewn samples and to admire the enticing new fabrics. Believe me, I help the local shops thrive. But there are never enough goodies for my appetite, so I often use mail-order and online quilting resources and services. Not only do I satisfy my quilting needs, but I also get to "visit" quilt stores I may never see in real life. I have ordered from, or received information from, each of the following resources, and I recommend them without hesitation.

For those of you who are hesitant about ordering online, the resources listed all have secure servers to protect your credit card information; however, if you are not convinced that this is safe, call with your order and credit card information. I have corresponded with each of them and have heard only excellent reviews from other online quilters.

BIGHORN QUILTS
529 Greybull Ave.
PO Box 566
Greybull, WY 82426
(877) 586-9150
www.bighornquilts.com

At the Worldwide Online Fabric Store, fabric takes center stage. Lots of it is at I-can't-resist prices.

CONNECTING THREADS
PO Box 8940
Vancouver, WA 98668-8940
(800) 574-6454
www.connectingthreads.com

Books and patterns take center stage in this catalog. A selection of rulers, rotary cutters, and many other quilting supplies are available, all at discounted prices. Call or write for a free mail-order catalog.

HANCOCK'S OF PADUCAH
3841 Hinkleville Road
Paducah, KY 42001
(800) 845-8723
www.Hancocks-Paducah.com

Hancock's of Paducah offers a delicious selection of the latest fabrics from the best manufacturers and designers, plus threads, quilting gadgets, batting, and more—all at great prices. Check out both the online and mail-order catalog; one may have fabrics that the other doesn't. Call, write, or visit the Web site to request a free catalog.

KEEPSAKE QUILTING
Route 25B
PO Box 1618
Centre Harbor, NH 03226-1618
(800) 865-9458
www.keepsakequilting.com

This hefty little catalog is chock-full of quilt notions, gadgets, patterns, books, and fabric, as well as handy fabric Medleys™. No wonder it is entitled, "The Quilter's Wishbook!" Call, write, or visit the Web site to request a free catalog.

PINE TREE QUILTWORKS, LTD.
585 Broadway
South Portland, ME 04106
(207) 799-7357
www.pinetree.quiltworks.com

Pine Tree Quiltworks, Ltd. offers everything a quilter needs, including a wonderful selection of fabrics, and every ruler and notion imaginable—all at discounted prices. Call, write, or visit the Web site to request a free catalog.

QUILT-A-WAY FABRICS
PO Box 163
Westminster Station, VT 05159
(802) 722-4743
www.quiltaway.com

A full service quilt shop, Quilt-a-way's mail-order site offers a great selection of fabrics at the lowest possible prices, including many batiks.

QUILTS AND OTHER COMFORTS
B2500
Louisiana, MO 63353-7500
(800) 881-6624
www.quiltsonline.com

"The catalog for quilt lovers" focuses on fabrics and patterns, with a good selection of popular books and wonderful quilt tools. Some nice gift-type items are featured as well. Call or visit the Web site to order a catalog.

EQUILTER.COM
4581 Maple Court
Boulder, CO 80301
(303) 516-1615
www.eQuilter.com

Specializing in Asian-Pacific and contemporary fabrics, eQuilter.com owner Luana Rubin worked throughout Asia as a textile and fashion designer and now brings her love of Asian textiles home to American quilters through her Web site.

>>> Tip <<<

When shopping for fabric online, I print out a picture of the fabric swatches so that I have a visual record of what I ordered. Then I staple the printout to my quilt design so that I remember exactly how I intended to use the fabric(s) in the quilt.

>>><<<

THE FOLLOWING ARE *a few starting points for exploring quilting and paper piecing in the wonderful world of cyberspace.*

PC PIECERS
bankswith.apollotrust.com/~larryb/PCPiecers.htm

Dedicated specifically to foundation piecing, the PC Piecers site has a lot of great information, patterns, and activities, as well as links to many other foundation-piecing sites and goodies.

ZIPPY DESIGNS PUBLISHING
Home of the *Foundation Piecer* Magazine
Rural Route 1, Box 187M
Newport, VA 24128
(888) 544-7153
www.zippydesigns.com

This magazine is devoted exclusively to foundation piecing. The creation of husband-and-wife team Elizabeth Schwartz and Stephen Seifert, the *Foundation Piecer* is a full-color magazine filled with inspiring patterns. Published six times a year, each issue contains eight to twelve projects.

The Web site for Zippy Designs is another great resource. Find foundation-piecing instructions, block patterns, information about the magazine and products, and much more at this site.

## Judy Smith's Quilting, Needlearts and Antiques Page
www.quiltart.com/judy

Judy is an online quilter who has used the Internet for a long time and has a highly acclaimed site of great quilting links. Start your search with Judy's site, and you will quickly accrue a long list of bookmarked favorites!

## About.com
www.quilting.about.com

The mission of About.com is to be *the* place to go to learn about any topic. Each area is devoted to a specific area of interest and is hosted by a real, live, accessible human being. The quilting area, hosted by Susan Druding, is a resource for all facets of quilting, offering how-to directions, answers to frequently asked questions, sources, links to other sites, and much more.

## Missing Fabrics Page
www.missingfabrics.com

The Missing Fabrics page works! I ran out of fabric for a quilt that started as a wall hanging and then I decided it had to be large enough for a bed. Because it had been produced two seasons before, no local or online shops had any of the fabric. So, I scanned it and posted it on the Missing Fabrics page. Lo and behold a quilter in Canada spotted it on the site and sent her friend, who lived closer to town, to fetch me some of the fabric from their local quilt shop.

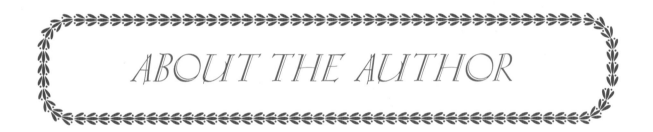

# ABOUT THE AUTHOR

JODIE DAVIS has been designing and sharing her designs for quilts, teddy bears, dolls, and cross-stitch for the last twelve years through the more than twenty books she has written. Having just moved to the hills north of Atlanta, Georgia, Yankee-born Jodie is thoroughly enjoying creating a new home with her husband, Bill; Domino, a Dalmatian; four cats; and Indy, her green-feathered studio buddy. She counts herself as truly lucky to work in the quilting world, which she proclaims is the only real world she believes in.

Visit Jodie online at www.iejodie.com.